GOLF TEES

TEEOGRAPHY

By Ken Jacobson

1

GOLF TEES

TEEOGRAPHY

Copyright © 2013 Ken Jacobson

FIRST EDITION

TEEOGRAPHY PRESS

18425 N. E. 95th St. #79 / Redmond, WA 98052 / 425.582.1205

GolfTeesTEEOGRAPHY.com

Jacobson, Ken

GOLF TEES TEEOGRAPHY

ISBN:9781484801826

1) Golf 2) Tees 3) Golf History 4) Golf Equipment 5) Patents 6) WOM 7) TEECUTTER

GOLF TEES TEEOGRAPHY

Table of Contents:

4	i.	ACKNOWLEDGEMENTS
6	ii.	FOREWORD
14	CHAPTER I	The Artificial Golf Tee…
20	CHAPTER II	The Earliest Tees
31	CHAPTER III	Who Invented the Tee?
46	CHAPTER IV	The First Commercial Tee
67	CHAPTER V	The "Classic" Lowell Tee Design
72	CHAPTER VI	The "Lowell" Family by Joan Lowell Smith
90	CHAPTER VII	The Brush-T by Richard Crouse
98	CHAPTER VIII	Over Three Billion Tees a Year
105	CHAPTER IX	400 Golf Tees – Classifications
110	CHAPTER X	Golf Ball History
114	CHAPTER XI	USGA, R&A and Golf Tee Rules
121	CHAPTER XII	USGA Decisions
126	CHAPTER XIII	New Rules of Golf
128	CHAPTER XIV	WOM Par 3 Golf Tee
131	CHAPTER XV	TEECUTTER
136	CHAPTER XVI	*"Tee it Down"* by Robert Trent Jones II
146		EPOLOGUE:
148		Author Profile:

ACKNOWLEDGEMENTS:

Writing a book exclusively about golf tees received a lot of comments, like… *"You're serious?"* and *"I didn't know there was enough information to write a book about tees?"*

GOLF TEE TEEOGRAPHY was a joy to research and to write. It was a dynamic experience that evolved after inventing two tees, the ALIGNMENT TEE (an insertion tee that indicates line-of-play) and the WOM ,a par 3 surface tee, a tee that is *retrievable, reshape-able and re-useable* and analyzing their market potential by gathering information about golf tees.

Originally, I believed there had never been a book exclusively about tees. Then I met Irv Valenta of Conroe, Texas, who was generous with his golf tee information. In 1995 he wrote and self-published a great book on tees (an edition of 800) … ***The Singular History of the Golf Tee.***

I was also fortunate to meet Joan Lowell Smith, a grand-daughter of Dr. William Lowell Sr., the inventor of the *"Reddy Tee"* which was the first successfully marketed wood tee. Joan is a writer and the family historian; She has all the detailed records of the Lowell family's 20 years of manufacturing and marketing to document her grandfather's, uncle's and father's efforts to make a success of the *"Reddy Tees"*. She also provided her written version of the Lowell family business to assure accurate interpretations for future generations.

Richard Crouse and his son Jason of Johannesburg Republic of South Africa, invented, designed and engineered the very successful and award-winning *"Brush-T"* that is based on the principle of *"driving a golf ball off fresh air"*. Richard's story takes us step-by-step through to creative process of bringing a new golf tee concept to market internationally.

Robert Trent Jones Jr. provided insight about the state of the art and future concerning golf course design. His talent, passion and concern for the growth of the game are evident in everything he is involved. His speech *"Tee it Down"* was presented to the American Society of Golf Course Architect in 2002. The substance of his proposal was made by Peter Dawson, Secretary of the R&A at the time, suggesting that we…

"Ban the artificial tee from the game and do it now!"

David Dawsey, I. P. Golf Guy provided both the U.S. and British patents to fill in gaps of designs that the author had not seen. Dawsey is a patent attorney with Gallager and Dawsey Co. LPA with offices in Cincinnati, Columbus and Dayton, Ohio. He has a love for the game of golf and everything associated with it. Golf-Patents.com blog is a must see for anyone who is interested in following what golf inventors are creating and what the industry leaders are doing related to intellectual property portfolios (patents and trademarks). His blog also follows litigation concerning the golf industry.

FOREWORD:

"Talk about humble beginnings... a pile of wet sand."

The development of the golf tee is the last significant change in the rules of golf. The simple little wooden tee may be golf's most innovative invention. It has affected golf courses, their length and design. It has affected the creation of the new technology used in the development of drivers, irons, shafts and golf balls. It has made playing golf easier and more enjoyable. It has provided the awe of long drives for professionals and amateurs alike.

The ruling authorities, the USGA and the R&A, did not define the golf tee in its rules until 2004.

There are numerous mentions and chapters in golf books on the subject of golf tees, but, at best there is very little information about the history of the golf tee. It appears this category of golfing history has been left unattended and underappreciated, probably viewed as lacking sufficient information, interest or importance. It may be they were viewed as being "illegal". The actions of the USGA over the past fifteen years concerning the development of the oversize high-technology drivers have increased the need and understanding of the use of these artificial golf tees.

During the past century, the simple golf tee has not gone unnoticed by golf tee inventors who have created over 400 golf tee designs. Over 300 individuals have thought enough of their inventions that they have spent the money to patent their golf tee. Based on all the prior rules of golf, by definition, they are artificial to the rules of golf. As such, the majority of the designs should have been illegal if used in competition prior to 2004.

GOLF TEES TEEOGRAPHY covers the history and evolution of the golf tee and design of golf tees since the first written Rules of Golf in 1744.

From the beginning of golf in 1472, tees were formed from natural substances… primarily dirt and sand from the hole of the immediate area next to the hole and from Mother Nature's natural materials. Such things as worm castings, dung, grass, etc. While there appears to be no clear written golf rules prior to 1744, there was a generally accepted method of playing the game.

There is much speculation and debate about who invented the artificial golf tee. Was the first tee a British Patent or a United States Patent? Was the first tee a "surface tee" or an "insertion tee"? Who invented the wooden tee? Who was the first to successfully market the golf tee? Many have claimed their tee was the "first".

Golf tees can be divided into two category types:

1) Surface Tees – that sit on the ground.
2) Insertion Tee – that are pushed into the ground.
   There is also a group of Novel Tees –(just for fun tees .)

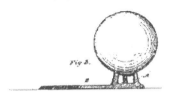

The first artificial tee, either Surface or Insertion, was a surface tee. A British Patent was issued to two Scotsmen, William Bloxsom and Arthur Douglas. Their design was a rubber platform with three posts. It even predated the first sand mold patent given to H. G. Alexander of Scotland and recorded in 1890.

The first insertion tee was also a British Patent in 1892 to Percy Ellis of England. It had a rubber top and metal spike and was commercially sold as the *"Perfectum"*.

Between 1889 (the first rubber & wood golf tee invention) and 1922 (the first successfully marketed golf tee) most golfers "ignored" all the new golf tee "patented inventions"…

"holding to the long honored rule that prohibited the use of any artificial aid to raise the ball from the ground".

The use and endorsement by golf professional celebrities in 1922 changed public perception and validated the "peg" as a much preferred alternative to piles of wet and dirty sand. The lack of enforcement of the artificial rule by USGA and R&A allowed the new wooden "Reddy Tee" to revolutionize the game of golf.

Factual documentation of golf tees and their history for **GOLF TEES TEEOGRAPHY** is sorted and incomplete, leaving much to speculation. Mostly, the information is from relatives, old golf rules, old articles, investigative analysis and deductive reasoning. Record keeping for an artificial device is rare, other than occasional mention in older (pre-1920) golf books. Much of the information is from over 300 British and US patents dating back to 1889. The patents provide reliable historic timelines, but do not allow detailed or documented follow-up because most new tee designs ended after receiving their patent when the inventor could not figure out how to market them. Some designs come from previous designs and others are manufactured tees that use or infringed on earlier designs. Many tees have been designed and manufactured without patents and were short lived.

The Royal and Ancient archives and the USGA libraries provided information on the constant changing of the Rules of Golf, but provided little information to document artificial tees.

GOLF TEES TEEOGRAPHY includes classification that divides Surface and Insertion Tees into two categories then separates them into similar families.

There are currently over 400 known golf tee designs.

The USGA was created in 1894 and the R&A followed in 1897. The Professional Golfers Association (PGA) was formed in 1914.

The first written Rules of Golf:

The first known rules of golf were drawn up for the World's First Open Golf Competition at Leith by the *Gentlemen Golfers of Edinburgh* in 1744. They would later become *The Honourable Company of Edinburgh Golfers.* Their original thirteen rules or articles became the foundation of the game of golf as we know it today.

Teeing a golf ball originally began in an area referred to as *"teeing grounds"* whereby the ball was placed on the ground or on a natural substance tee within one club length of the previous hole. Many individual clubs made different rules that pertained specifically to their members play. Today, teeing grounds are called *"tee boxes"* or "tees" and can be located a great distance from the previous hole.

To add to the vagaries of the game of golf, the word ***"tee"*** has multiple meanings and can be used as two nouns, a verb or adjective when describing the game. Ie:

*"Starting at each **tee** there are eighteen opportunities to **tee** your ball on a **tee** from a **tee**."*

The multiple uses of the word ***"tee"*** can lead to confusion among non-golfers and those not familiar with the jargon of golf. "Tee" as a noun is used both as a "peg", "golf tee" or "wooden, plastic, rubber, etc. tee". Used as a verb "tee" can mean to "place" or "tee" the ball on a tee. As an adjective, it can be used to describe a golf shot, ie: identifying a "tee shot". There are also Men's Tees; Women's Tees; Tee Time and Pro Tees.

The early dictionaries are the most historical correct information of the creation of the word "tee". They state its origins and its universal acceptance. The Scottish have been playing the game of golf and curling for centuries. As such, without documentation to the contrary, credit for the use of the word "tee" can and probably should be given to the Scottish.

Dictionary definitions:

A *"tee"* is a stand to support a stationary ball.

Tee – Pronunciation Key *n*

1. The letter *t*.

2. Something shaped like a T

3. Sports & Games. A mark aimed at in certain games, such as curling or quoits. Back-information from obsolete Scot **teaz** (taken as a pl.)

Included in the common terms of the Curling glossary...

Tee is the cross in the button.

Button is the small center of the circles.

Quoits is a game in which flat rings of iron or rope are pitched at a stake (or tee), with points awarded for encircling it.

tee – Pronunciation Key *(te)*

> 1. A small peg with a concave top for holding a golf ball for an initial drive.
> 2. The designated area of each golf hole from which a player makes his or her first stroke.
> 3. A device used to stand a football on end for a kickoff.
> 4. A shaft with a concave top attached to a flat base, used to hold the ball in T-ball.

teed, tee-ing, tees

To place (a ball) on a tee. Often used with *up*.

Phrasal Verb:
tee off

> 1. To drive a golf ball from the tee.

2. _Slang_ To start or begin: *They teed off the fundraising campaign with a dinner.*

3. _Slang_ To make angry or disgusted: *The impertinent remarks teed the speaker off.*

The obvious conclusion is that since sand and dirt were originally a part of the *"teeing ground"*, they were usually taken from the hole or immediate area to build a tee mound. This area would become known as a *"tee"*. The proximity of the *"teeing ground"* to the hole, or *"tee"* as the Old Scots called it during curling makes perfect sense. Adding sand boxes on each teeing ground or requiring caddies to carry moist sand, were simply the results of the increased popularity of the game.

CHAPTER I

The Artificial Golf Tee...

The Biggest Change in Golfing History

In 1921, a massive revolution took place in golf. For almost five centuries, golfers had used dirt or sand to tee up the golf ball. That all changed with the arrival of the wood insertion tee – the predecessor of the modern tee that most golfers use today.

"The wood insertion tee, as an invention, is as important to golf as the wheel was to the mobility of man."

All the modern innovations in the game, including two-piece balls, perimeter weighting, titanium heads and graphite shafts, etc. have not had the same impact collectively, as the simple wooden tee.

There are two vectors in golf – distance and direction. Since the introduction of the wooden tee, golf innovators and entrepreneurs have come up with over 400 tee designs that have promised golfers more distance with longer drives.

I know this because I have also invented an alignment tee and was excited about the prospects of marketing it. Unfortunately, in 2003, I presented a tee design to USGA which turned my ALIGNMENTEE down as an illegal "non-conforming" product. "Non-conforming" is a simple USGA catch-all term for rejection. In 2004 USGA officially initiated a new rule 11-1 in their rules book that restricted my ALIGNMENT tee design to a practice or training aid.

The new rule outlined what would define the criteria for a legal golf tee stating the golf tee cannot indicate direction. Yet, they allow directional lines on drivers, irons, balls and putters… What are their criteria for making these conflicting determinations?

I have perhaps the largest private collection of golf tee designs in the world. I have the United States and British patents as well as other unique designs I have collected over the years.

Some people collect clubs. Some people collect golf balls. I collect golf tee designs and I have collected more information about tee designs (400 plus) than anyone I know. The results of my obsession with golf tee designs (while not intentionally the goal) became the contents of this book.

The history of Golf Tees fascinates me, because it's also an unattended part of the history of golf. Golf Tees have been blinked and neglected by the governing bodies for the past century, probably because of the important financial role golf equipment plays in the industry. The driver is big business and who doesn't like to hit the ball a long way or watch long drives?

The golf tee provides a rare insight into the mind and motivations of the golf entrepreneur. It also provides insight into how golf's ruling bodies operate and decide how to organize and interpret the rules. So while the tee may be an afterthought for most golfers who simply pick them up en masse in a golf shop or their club's pro shop, this small but essential device has a long, fascinating and storied history.

Even today, golf entrepreneurs are trying to reinvent the tee. At a PGA Merchandise Show in Orlando, several companies offered variations on the theme… flavored tees; biodegradable tees; plastic tees with bristles on top. Nothing will deter the imagination of man and his relentless desire to create new products and a better golf tee. They come up with claims offering a golf tee offering better accuracy and more distance. However, nobody has broken through the market in a massive way, except the simple original design that Dr. William Lowell Sr., created in 1921 and patented in 1924, which is still the fundamental wood tee design that the majority of golfers use today.

There are some great exceptions that find a path to success. The Brush-T award-winning creation is an industrial design work of art with packaging to match. It received approval from both USGA and R&A. It had great attention to detail and is an internationally marketed golf tee based on the principle that you are *"driving off fresh air"*.

Some tees are unbelievable… My favorite unusual golf tee invention is a tee that you wind up. The inventors patent was based on the concept that a moving ball would help the golfer keep his *"eye on the ball"* ???

Of the 300 plus tee designs with patents, only a handful made it to the manufacturing stage. Very few of these inventors, designers or entrepreneurs have enjoyed huge financial success for their efforts. Most have failed for the usual reasons – lack or interest or financing or costs were too high and sales volume was too low.

The ruling bodies have also erected hurdles, primarily through the stipulation that any equipment that is "non-conforming" be brought before the powers-that-be for approval. And when it comes to tees almost everything seems to be "non-conforming". These are the same bodies that allowed metal to replace wood drivers; branding irons to replace putters; and directional lines on all golf equipment except tees.

It wasn't until 2004 that the USGA officially recognized the tee as a separate piece of equipment and initiated some regulations, including limiting the length of the tee to no more than four inches. The rules about tees are vague, complicated and open to wide interpretation which, based on my experience with the USGA is just how they like it. For example, the USGA stipulates that no tee can "indicate line of play" or "influence the movement of the ball", yet the language is (perhaps deliberately) wishy-washy and confusing, especially to those who are interested in designing a better tee.

Can a unique and innovative tee design help golfers get better results? That's a difficult question to answer as most of the patented designs never made it to manufacturing to be tested. You don't have to have USGA approval to get a patent. You do have to get their approval to use them in a USGA event or sanctioned competition that uses USGA rules. Many clubs handicapping requires following their local rules combined with USGA rules. So, technically you would be in violation if you used equipment not approved by USGA if your club chose to strictly enforce "the rules".

Perhaps the fact that the USGA finally defined and made some rules about the tee is proof that somebody is onto something that could significantly help golfers hit the ball straighter and further?

The USGA, within certain parameters, has let ball and club manufactures make great strides with equipment, especially in the last twenty years. And these technologies have made the game more enjoyable for golfers of all standards. It's difficult to understand why they have not let tee manufactures get into the game. After all, the current tee is a massive improvement over the old method of placing the ball of a small mound of sand or dirt. Imagine how much more fun they might have with a new tee design that helps hit the ball straighter and longer.

Despite the new restrictive rules, golf entrepreneurs are still going to try to bring new and innovative tees to the market, primarily because there is potential for financial gain. It is also just plain fun to invent around a game you love. Golfers use over three-billion tees a year; the business person who can re-invent the tee and get a chunk of this market should do very well. The fact is, over the past ninety years, few of the 300 plus patents have made golfers change en masse. In the mid-1990's, every golfer had metal spikes on their golf shoes. Today, only a handful of professionals still use them.

So, enjoy your journey into a small part of the world of the simple little golf tee…

the Biggest Change in Golf History.

I call it **GOLF TEES TEEOGRAPHY**.

CHAPTER II

The Earliest Tees

The earliest golf courses in Scotland and the rest of the British Isles were, in today's golf vernacular, *goat tracks.* To be more precise, they were coastal sheep and cattle grazing grounds complete with sandy waste areas, marshes, burns, natural bunkers, a variety of grasses and all types of imperfections including worm casts, ruts and various types of ordure. The first recorded reference to golf courses comes from 1457 when James II of Scotland banned golf because he felt that it was interfering with archery practice. The exact proclamation:

"The Fut Ball and Goff be utterly cryit dune."

Football (Fut Ball) or soccer as it's known in the United States has thrived worldwide and so has golf. So, thankfully, at least a few of the archers that James II addressed decided to ignore the edict.

The links from three centuries ago and beyond bear little relation to today's modern well-maintained and well-defined courses. Just about everything has changed. The Old Course at St. Andrews had 18 holes eventually, but most early courses were based purely on the number of holes suitable for them from the ground available. Some had six holes. Others had twelve. Some courses had more than 18. It all depended on space and the whims of the locals who played the game at the time. The St. Andrews Links in Scotland occupy a narrow strip of land along the sea. St. Andrews golfers, as early as the 15th Century, established routes through the undulating terrain and played holes dictated by the topography. The course featured eleven holes stretched from the clubhouse to the end of the property. The holes were played outward, turned around and played the holes inward totaling twenty-two holes. In 1764, several holes were considered too short and were combined reducing the number of holes to nine so that a round totaled 18 holes. Golf courses today have 18 holes because that's the number of holes on the Old Course at St. Andrews and once golf went inland and became more standardized; everyone simply copied the Old Course at St. Andrews.

"One Club Length from the Previous Hole"

Originally, early golfers started the next hole immediately adjacent to the hole they had just played; the official distance was a club length or less from the hole. That's quite a difference from today when a teeing ground can be several hundred yards from the preceding green and hole. The "one club length" rule changed to two clubs (and more) from the hole and eventually, most courses had an official teeing ground that was immediately adjacent to the last green. That's one reason why, on most of the older English and Scottish golf courses, the next tee is just a few yards from the preceding green.

Nobody knows exactly when or where golfers started to tee the ball up, but this likely happened in the mid 1700s when some formalization of the game and rules began. However, one set of the rules in 1744 states that *"Your Tee must be upon the ground."* This may have indicated that certain golfing scoundrels were raising the ball off the ground, thus creating what some must have deemed as an unfair advantage.

Why did they want to raise the ball for the first shot? With a general improvement in equipment, some players found it easier to tee off by elevating the ball off the ground. Those early golfers, like today's golfers, wanted more distance with the club they used to tee off and found that they hit the ball further with a clean strike if they raised if off the ground.

Sand and Dirt

Early tees looked nothing like today's tees. That's because early tees weren't really tees at all, but simply a small pile of sandy soil scooped out of the last hole. When the hole became too scooped out, the golfers on that course dug a new hole. The word *"tee"* likely comes from the sport of curling. In curling, the line through the center of the target circle is also called *"the tee"*. And because the earliest golf teeing ground was within a circle of the hole, the word "tee" likely moved easily from curling to golf.

The next step in the evolution of the tee took place when players or caddies took a small leather pouch with them when they played; the pouch contained wet sand as this substance made for the most consistent tee. Soon, in lieu of the pouch, some coursed put small sand boxes immediately adjacent to the tee. These were also called *"tee boxes"*. There would also be water available to moisten the sand on the rare occasions in Scotland when it was not raining horizontally.

For several decades, fashioning the sand into a tee was not only an art, or at least a craft, but a source of some debate. Harry Vardon, the Champion Scottish golfer, liked a low and inconspicuous tee. A contemporary of Vardon's, W. P. Park, liked the ball teed up. As you will discover later in this book, there is still debate among professionals and golf's ruling bodies as to the benefits of teeing it up or teeing it low.

Clues from the Development of the Rules

Early sets of the rules of golf provide the best clues as to the early history of the tee. *The Gentlemen Golfers* of Leith and subsequently the *Honorable Company of Edinburgh Golfers* authored perhaps the first set of official rules for the game. When golfers at Leith and in Edinburgh started to write their own rules, the *Royal and Ancient Golf Club of St. Andrews* had not yet taken over as the official mastodon of rule making and so the rules were constantly changing; rules varied significantly from course to course. It would have been interesting to be a *"mouse in the corner"* witnessing the clashing and king making of egos and opinions when those early golfers were coming up with initial regulations. Perhaps it was more of the gentlemanly affair with fraternal discussion and banter over a long meal with plenty of good claret.

As stated earlier, a set of rules from 1744 indicate that there was some dissention over how and where to tee the ball. The earliest rules of golf were drafted on March 7th 1744 for a tournament played on April 2nd in Leith. There were thirteen "articles". The first three were....

Rule 1 required…
"Your must tee your ball within a club length of the hole."

Rule 2 required…
"Your tee must be upon the Ground."

Rule 3 declared…
"You are not to change the ball you strike off the tee."

Thus the golfers in Leith declared a very specific set of rules to play their game of golf. And they were very specific about defining the concept of the tee. And if someone wasn't gaining some sort of advantage by teeing the ball *"off the ground"*, then why did the people at Leith insist that the tee be *"upon"* the ground and did that automatically preclude the use of sand for a tee?

In 1773, a new rule stated *"no ball shall be teed nearer the hole than two club lengths, nor farther from it than four."* However, the origin of this rule is not clear.

Soon afterwards, the Honorable Company (later the *Royal Burgess Golfing Society*) made a rule *"forbidding tees made from anything within ten yards of the hole"*. These particular rule-makers initiated this rule because the hole was likely becoming too big with too many people scooping out too much dirt to make tees. The new rule also called for new holes to be cut on medal days, when all putts had to holed-out. Today, at all clubs in Scotland, medal days are especially important because these are competition days. The greens keeper cuts new holes and play takes place from the hallowed ground of the medal tee, which cannot be used for informal routine play – even if your first name is Jack and your last name is Nicklaus.

Where there's Smoke, there is Fire

Golf rule making continued. The rules specifically pertaining to tees and the teeing ground not only helped to define these important parts of the game, but they also provide verbal evidence that certain golfers were attempting to do certain things to gain an advantage.

In 1776, rule 2 of the *Honorable Company of Edinburgh Golfers* stated…

"Your tee must be on the ground and unconnected with any conductor or leader to the ball."

The Honorable Company of Edinburgh Golfers likely initiated this rule to prohibit the use of any artificial aid to raise the ball from the ground; they probably wanted tees to be made of sand and dirt from the ground and nothing else. This rule is the forerunner of today's rule that bans the use of artificial devices and unusual equipment. Had the USGA and R&A enforced this rule at the beginning of the twentieth century, it would never have allowed pegs on teeing grounds and the modern tee might never have emerged.

In 1977, the *Society of St. Andrews Golfers* passed this resolution…

"None of the Society shall tee their golf balls within less than a play club length of the hole from which they are to strick off, nor at a greater distance than four lengths of said club from hole."

The society maintained this rule until 1812

The *Crail Golfing Society*, in 1786, adopted a rule that kept the player from making a welt in the turf with his heel or club, requiring the player *"Not to break the ground on the teeing of his ball"*. Other clubs adopted the rule, but the R&A, the Honorable Company and other Edinburgh clubs did not seem concerned about this type of activity.

Slowly but surely, the tee started to move further and further away from the hole. In 1824, Thistle Golf Club stipulated that the distance become *"between two and six club lengths"*.

Perth Golf Club in 1825 moved the distance to six to ten club lengths.

R&A in 1851 it was between six and eight club lengths.

The development of the teeing ground continued as the St. Andrews golfers elevated themselves to become the Royal and Ancient Golf Club of St. Andrews in 1851. Most importantly, they gave the teeing ground a name: ***"A place called the tee."***

Then the first mention of the "Teeing Grounds" and markers... R&A in 1875 moved the distance to between eight and twelve club lengths.

At this stage of the game's development, it should be noted that there is no record of anyone using anything other than soil for a tee, although, the very wording of some of the rules indicate possible artificial indiscretions. Also, it seems that some enterprising caddies were starting to offer additional services, specifically carrying wet sand.

R&A in 1882, declared the teeing ground was indicated by markers with a depth of two club lengths.

R&A in 1891, they stipulated a rectangular shape for the teeing ground for the first time requiring the golfer to place his ball within the rectangular shape.

In 1829, *Musselburgh Golf Club* adopted the rule of not taking sand or soil within ten yards of the hole and then, in 1839, banned any *"Cady… who does not carry a bag of moist sand or clay for the tees".*

One of the first golf books, *The Golfers Manual*, published in 1857, defines "tee" as *"A pat of soil on which the ball is elevated for the first stroke".*

Further Defining the Tee

The 1875 revision of the rules established a separate teeing ground.

The ball must be teed and not be nearer the hole than eight nor further than twelve club lengths, except where special ground has been marked by the Conservator of the Links, which shall be considered the 'Teeing Ground' and the balls shall be teed within and not in advance of such marks."

Thus the R&A established, or let the 'Conservator of the Links' establish, a totally separate teeing ground. The person responsible for this change may have been (Old) Tom Morris who established separate teeing areas on the Old Course at St. Andrews. Old Tom Morris was appointed Conservator of the links in 1864. He created the 18th green in 1865 and the first hole in 1870. He also created smooth, true putting surfaces around the holes in the early 1880's and sited teeing ground separately for the putting greens.

Further changes soon arrived. The 1882 and 1888 R&A rules stated…

"The ball must be teed within the marks laid down by the Conservator of the Links, which shall be considered the "Teeing Ground". The balls shall not be teed in advance of such marks, nor more than two club lengths behind them."

Thus we have the introduction of the tee markets and also the *"box"* behind those – a concept still in use today. In 1891, the R&A further refined the rule to read…

"The teeing ground shall be indicated by two marks placed in a line at right angles to the course, and the player shall not tee in front of, nor on either side of, these marks, nor more than two club lengths behind them. A ball played from outside the limits of the teeing ground, as thus defined, may be recalled by the opposite side."

This version of the rule now includes a penalty. From 1891 to 1952 the rules remained mostly the same only with slightly different penalties for breach of the rule. In 1952, the R & A and the USGA combined their rules to require the player to…

"Count that stroke and any subsequent stroke so played and then play from within the teeing ground with the privilege of teeing the ball.

A potentially serious penalty!

The First 'Artificial' Tee in the Rules

The first indication in the rules of golf that a large number of golfers were no longer using just sand and adjuncts perhaps came in 1908 when the rule officially defined teeing the ball.

"In 'teeing', the ball may be placed on the ground or on sand or other substance in order to raise it off the ground."

Finally, in 1984, the rule makers moved the tee from the definitions part of the rule book to the main structure specifically the beginning of Rule 11-1. The slight change provided official recognition for the noun version of **"tee,"** specifically indicating that the ball can be placed *"on the ground, or an irregularity of surface created by the player on the ground or on a tee, sand or other substance"*. However, the word "tee" still lacked a specific definition in the rules. This would ultimately change in 2004. Until that point, the rules treated the inserted elevated wooden golf tree as an incidental and abstract aid, left to the vagaries and vicissitudes of R&A and USGA determinations and definitions. These organizations mentioned the tee in their rule books only in relationship to the teeing ground.

In 1908 the rule stated that the ball may be placed on the ground or on the sand or other substance… additionally in 1980, on an irregularity of surface and eventually in 1984 *"on a tee"*. The movement away from sand and dirt tees to the wood insertion tee and other devices was a pivotal moment in golf. And without tees, and today's modern teeing ground, golf would be a significantly different game. Despite the importance of the tee, the governing bodies of the game have paid little attention to it until the adoption of their 2004 Rule 11.1.

The First 'Artificial' Tees

Who was the first person to have that *"ah-ha"* moment when they slapped their self on the forehead and decided that there was a better faster way to tee the ball than wet and and/or dirt?

CHAPTER III

Who Invented the Tee?

With golf becoming more popular in the last decade of the 19th Century, fashioning a tee from sand, dirt and water became somewhat of an irritant. It was messy and also took some time. And in Scotland, playing golf quickly is undertaken with a quasi-religious zeal.

The first significant change in teeing the ball up was the arrival of the conically-shaped mold that created a well defined surface tee. This sped up the process of making a tee and also made the tee more consistent. The process was not unlike a small child filling a small bucket of sand at the beach then simply turning it over to make what might be parapet for a sand castle. Molds (or "moulds" in the United Kingdom) came in different heights for different clubs. H. G. Alexander of Scotland recorded the first patent for a sand mold tee in 1890. However, William Gibson Bloxsom of Cromwell Lodge, North Berwick and Arthur Sherwood Douglas of Edinburgh received the first patent for any type of tee, mould or otherwise.

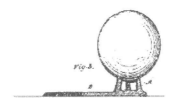

1890 – Bloxsom/Douglas Surface Tee

31

The Bloxsom/Douglas tee was a surface tee. The golfer put the tee *on* the ground (as opposed to *in* the ground). The tee comprised of a rubber platform with three protruding fingers to support the ball. There was also a directional arrow probably for correct alignment. The date of the application for the patent was the 16th of August, 1889.

So which came first, the mold or the surface tee? The question and the answer are perhaps moot because the tee type that we use today is the insertion tee. The printed patent record, recorded the Bloxsom/Douglas tee was the first artificial tee for the game of golf. So, until someone can prove the existence of an earlier tee, and document it, **GOLF TEES TEEOGRAPHY** will consider it to be the first artificial golf tee.

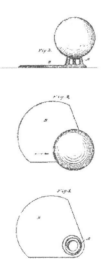

1890 Bloxsom/Douglas Surface Tee

Mold-type tees are no longer used except in vintage tournaments where golfer return to the 1920's or earlier and play older courses using antique clubs while wearing knickers.

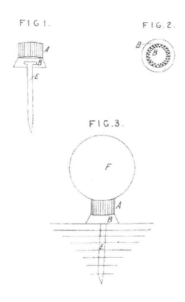

1892 – *"Perfectum"* Insertion Tee

The first insertion tee to appear in golf journals in the United Kingdom was the *"Perfectum"* tee which comprised a small spike and a series of small rubber studs to support the ball. While the initial advertising list Mssrs. Thompson and Company of 147 Queen Victoria Street as the people selling the product, Percy Ellis received the patent for the device in the United Kingdom on February 29th 1892. The copy in the advertisement touts several benefits: less resistance; durability; no more mess from sand tees; and no need to carry any more tees.

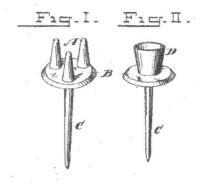

1897 – Matthews Insertion Tee

In 1897, Patrick Millar Matthews of Scotland introduced a cup-shaped rubber head on a peg and received a patent for the device on the 12th June 1897.

First in America

The first United States patent for a tee came not from the United States but from Scotland. In 1895, David Dalziel of Glasgow received a patent for a rubber tee with artificial turf – a surface tee to be permanently set in the ground.

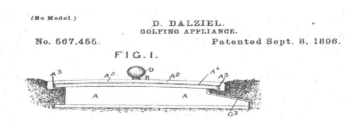

The first American to receive a tee patent was Prosper L. Senat of Philadelphia who received his patent on November 3rd 1896. Senat's design was an interesting combination of scorecard and tee, the golfer simply folded the die-cut scorecard into a tee! Soon after, on November 21st, 1898, A. Sewal of Boston patented a rubber washer and ball seat that, like Senat's tee, was a surface tee.

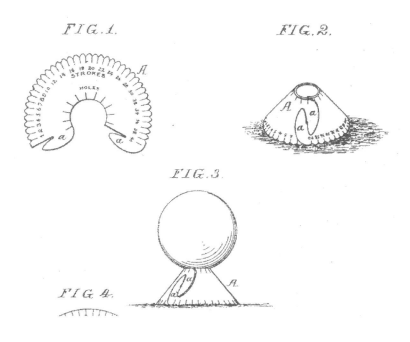

1896 – Prosper L. Senat's Surface Tee
The First *"American Designed"* Golf Tee

Dr. Grant's Patent

The most significant patent was the next one. On December 12, 1899, Dr. George Franklin Grant, a Boston dentist, received a patent for an insertion tee with a wood base and a rubber head. Grant's concept was a simple one that he never marketed, mostly because golfers didn't care for it; Grant simply gave some to his friends for their personal use.

Many authorities have written about the original tee describing Grant's invention as "wooden" or "a wooden peg". Some have written that it didn't have a concave head suggesting that the design was flawed or that it was all-wood construction. Grant's tee was actually a combination tee that used wood as its pointed base to insert into the ground and a rubber top that let the ball to nest on it. Grant possibly got the rubber tube section from his dental office.

A careful analysis of his patent suggests the tee might have been clumsy or not rigid enough to penetrate harder ground. Whether commercially successful or not, Grant's tee is important because it was the original concept in the United States for a wooden insertion golf tee. It was the forerunner of the tee that millions of golfers have used and continue to use today. Grant has justifiably received attention for his invention. In 1991, the USGA finally acknowledged the Grant patent as the first "wooden" tee.

The official patent number was #638,920. Grant believed it promoted longer drives. The patent describes the tee as…

"A rigid base portion and attached flexible head, the base being preferably made of wood and tapering to a point at its lower end to be readily inserted in the ground (tee had a rubber head with annual seat) on which the ball rested as in a cup… when the ball is struck, the head will yield in the direction of the travel of the ball, offering no obstruction to its flight."

It was the world's first patent for a wood and rubber golf tee.

Dr. George F. Grant (1847 -1910) graduated from Harvard Dental School in 1870. He was one of the first two African Americans to graduate from Harvard Dental School where he later taught. He was born in Oswego, New York and was the son of former slaves.

Grant eventually became interested in playing golf and the usual method of teeing, involving sand and water and the requisite mess, appeared to annoy him. Although his invention made teeing the ball much easier and cleaner, the invention was not widely received. Why Dr. Grant did not market his tee is unknown. Some believed its use would be illegal. He did have a small number of his tees produced locally and gave them to friends and other golfers.

While it's clear that Grant's invention was extremely valuable to golfers, his greater contribution to mankind was his other invention – the oblate palate. This was a prosthetic device he designed for the treatment of the cleft palate. In dental circles, he is internationally known for this invention. One of Grant's patients was Charles W. Eliot, a one-time president of Harvard.

No. 638,920.

Patented Dec. 12, 1899.

G. F. GRANT.
GOLF TEE.
(Application filed July 1, 1899.)

(No Model.)

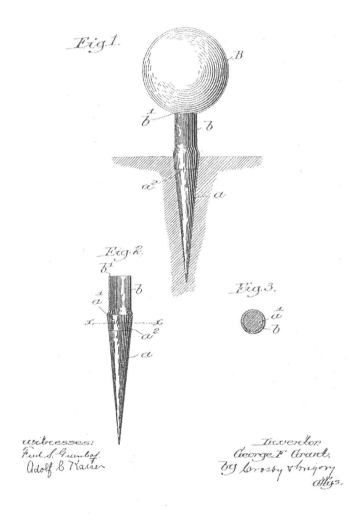

Fig.1

Fig.2.

Fig.3.

Witnesses:
Fred S. Greenleaf.
Adolf C. Kaiser

Inventor
George F. Grant,
By Crosby & Gregory
Attys.

38

1899 - Dr. George F. Grant's Wood & Rubber Insertion Tee

George F. Grant – Patent 638,920

UNITED STATES PATENT OFFICE

George F. Grant, of Boston, Massachusetts

GOLF TEE

SPECIFICATION forming part of Letters Patent No. 638,920, dated December 12, 1899. Application filed July 1, 1899. Serial No. 722,500 (No Model)

To whom it may concern:

Be it know that I, GEORGE F. GRANT, of Boston, County of Suffolk, State of Massachusetts, have invented an Improvement in Golf Tees, of which the following description, in connection with the accompanying drawings, is a specification, like letters on the drawings representing like parts.

This invention has for its object the production of a simple, cheap, and effective tee for the use in the game of golf, obviating the use of the usual conical mounds of sand or similar material formed by the fingers of the player on which the ball is supported when driving off.

While the tee must firmly, yet lightly, support the ball until hit by the player's club, the tee must be so constructed that it will not in any manner interfere with the swing or *"carry through"* of the club in making the stroke. These requisites are possessed in full by my invention, and the annoyance and sometimes discomfort attendant upon the formation of a sand tee are obviated thereby.

Fig. 1 Represents a golf-tee embodying one form of my invention, shown as inserted in the ground and supporting a ball ready to be struck. **Fig. 2** is a side elevation of the base portion of the tee, the head being shown in section; and **Fig. 3** is a transverse section 30 on the line **xx, Fig. 2**

In accordance with my invention the tee comprises a rigid base portion a and an attached flexible head b, the base being preferably made of wood and tapering to a point at its lower end to be readily inserted in the ground. Near its upper end the base is preferably reduced in diameter, as at **a1**, to leave an annular shoulder **a2**, and over the reduced portion is stretched one end of a piece of rubber tubing forming the head b. the tubing being drawn down to the shoulder **a2**. I prefer to cement the head to the base around the part **a1** of the latter, the open upper end of the head presenting an annual seat **b1**, in which the ball **B** rests as in a cup, as shown in **Fig 1**.

In practice the base is driven into the ground to substantially the shoulder **a2**, the head projecting upward about three-quarters of an inch. When the ball is struck, the head will yield in the direction of travel of the ball, offering no obstruction to its flight, and if the club strikes the head, as will frequently be the case, the yield will not in any way retard or stop the proper swing of the club as it is carried through the stroke.

The tee may be withdrawn after the drive and again used for the next drive, and so on, or the tee may remain permanently in the tee-ing ground, as desired or fund more convenient.

By the use of the tee, as described, the player is sure that his ball is uniformly elevated from the ground at each drive and the uncertainty of a sand tee is overcome, as it is practically impossible to make them of uniform height each time.

Having fully described my invention, what I claim, and desire to secure by Letters Patent, is…

1. As an article of manufacture, a golf-tee comprising a tapering base portion to be driven into the ground point first, and a flexible tubular head, the lower end of which embraces the upper tapering portion of the base.
2. As an article of manufacture, a golf-tee comprising a tapering base portion adapted to be inserted in the ground pint first and having a shoulder near its upper end, a tubular head, the lower end of which embraces the tapering base portion above the shoulder.

In testimony whereof I have signed my name to this specification in the presence of two subscribing witnesses.

GEORGE F. GRANT
Witnesses: John C. Edwards, Emma J. Bennett

The First Golf Tee Patent Rush

Between 1890 and 1920 a motley crew of inventors came up with over 50 patents for golf tees. The number of patents would increase almost exponentially after 1920, but a look at the first wave of tee patents reveals some interesting designs and curious advertising. Clearly, several entrepreneurs thought they could make a pile of cash by replacing the pile of sand that had sufficed for a tee for several centuries. These entrepreneurs were the first to think this way, but they would not be the last!

These entrepreneurs and inventors came up with any number of interesting names for their products to complement the product and get it to move off the shelves or out of the warehouse. For example, the *"Springboard Tee"* was a launching pad of sorts featuring an elevated metal prong; the ball rested on the end of the prong and the golfer could likely get away with hitting several inches behind the ball as the club could spring into the ball along the prong. Many of the early devices look like instruments for medieval dental or nasal torture. Some of these original tees still exist in golf museums around the world.

Early insertion and surface tee, plus sand molds, varied from the simple to excessively complex. The inventors focused on the benefits of their products.

The Matthews Tee Mould even berated the caddies for not being able to build consistent tees.

"It is not every caddie that can make a tee. The erections on which some caddies place the ball are more like bunkers than tees, and even those

who have mastered the art fairly well are apt to vary their height, while much time is lost in the process of constructing the edifice."

The person who wrote the copy for the *"Perfectum"* Tee said that it was a *"novelty"* but also points out that *"No damage is done to the club should the tee be accidentally struck."*

The manufacturers of the *"Star"* Tee could have used the services of a better illustrator, but touted some interesting features and benefits. *One*, it's impossible to lose it. *Two*, the ball will not roll off the tee. *Three*, it's virtually indestructible.

One advertisement for *"Ransome's Double Golf Tee Stamp"*, a mold tee, includes a testimonial, albeit and unsigned one.

"I am greatly pleased with the stamp you sent me and shall advise all my golfing friends to get one."

High praise indeed.

Some tee producers distributed through well-known sporting stores while others went directly to the consumer.

Early American Tees

American golf entrepreneurs from 1890-1910 also tried to establish their tee designs in the market. The United States Patent Office issued well over 30 patents for tees from 1896 to 1918. The inventors came from all over the United States, showing that golf was spreading rapidly through the country. M. Fuchs of Baker, Oregon got a patent for a tee specifically for the driving range. B. R. Benjamin of Oak Park, Illinois got a patent for a paper tee.

And C. G. Duganne got a patent for a cardboard tee. Other serious inventors came from Vermont, Massachusetts, Pennsylvania, New York, Ohio, and Michigan.

The range and scope of these early tees varied significantly.

H. E. Wetzel's design comprised of rolled up waxed paper and stiffened cloth.

C. E. Stockader made his tee out of *"finely bolted sand, powdered clay, flour, salt-water and molasses"*.

The *"Nice Tee"*; *"All-My-Tee"*; *"No Looz"*; *"Excel"* and similar designs were made out of weighted rubber. Many tee manufactures produced tethered tees to restrain the tee from flying all over the course. Like other designs, these tees had interesting names" "Noveltee"; "Line-a-Tee"; "Rubber Neck", etc. One design was made of sterling silver.

American tee advertising has some interesting / presumptuous copy:

The *"Angle Tee"*... And what a tee it is!

The *"Dodo Tee"*... For a long Straight Drive!

The Patented *"Cutoyut"* Makes a good stroke perfect... speeds up the game...

"Perfectee"... More than simply a ball-stand – scientifically designed to direct the club head to the center of the ball...

Ready for the "Reddy Tee"

Although patent records clearly indicate who was first past the post with patents for surface, mold and insertion tees in the United States and the United Kingdom, there is no clear proof of any one individual inventor being the absolute first person to come up with the idea for a better tee than wet sand.

However, in the early 1920's, it was absolutely clear who became the first person set up a viable and successful commercial wood and plastic tee manufacturing and distribution business. That person was Dr. William Lowell Sr. marketing the Lowell family's "Reddy Tees".

CHAPTER IV

The First
Commercially Successful Tee

Despite the introduction and proliferation of interesting and innovative tees in the years preceding and following the turn of the century, golfers in the 1920s were still using sand and water to make tees. None of the inventors had enjoyed any degree of commercial impact. So, upon arrival at the tee, golfers would go to the "tee box" where they would find sand and water; they then began the job of constructing a small suitable mound. If they were lucky, a golfer might have a mold. At the Maplewood Golf Club in New Jersey, Dr. William Lowell Sr., a dentist, was just beginning his journey into golf (he was originally a tennis player), but now, in his late 50s, he decided to take up the game.

According to Lowell's granddaughter Joan Lowell Smith, Lowell was serious enough about his sports to *dress up* rather than down. He played his first rounds of golf dressed immaculately in white plus-fours and fully intended to remain immaculate throughout the round. He thus found the messy business of tee building to be just that, *messy*, and quickly tried to find another way to tee the ball. He visited the top sports stores in New York City hoping to find a suitable alternative to using sand and water. He found nothing that he liked.

In his memoirs, Lowell's son, also named William, wrote that the lack of a suitable alternative frustrated his father.

"Father was incredulous that there was nothing to replace sand mounds. Not easily put off, in a blinding flash of creativity, he raced to his South Orange office to whittle the first tee from a stick or a small parade flag then molding gutta percha on the top to form a concavity for the ball. He used this as a prototype which he had a wood-turner replicate in wood."

It was instantly clear to Lowell (and his sons) that he had stumbled across something that would not only change the game significantly but also have some commercial merit. Golf was a red-hot sport. In 1913, Francis Ouimet's victory in Boston at the U.S. Open captured the nation's imaginations. Americans were buying balls, clubs, clothes and a host of accessories. Golf course architects like Donald Ross were so busy that they had to hire hundreds of workers to build courses all over the United States. The potential for a tee that solved the sand/water/messy hands issue was massive.

Lowell and his sons refined the product and tested their new tee. It worked. It could pierce the ground easily. The golfer could tee the ball at varying heights for different clubs. It held the ball well in the wind. It was invisible to the golfer. It was light and easy to carry. It was clean. And it had no effect on the direction of the ball.

Initially, according to his granddaughter's account, Lowell was not especially interested in turning his invention into a commercial enterprise. However, his sons, one of whom was a sporting goods buyer for Marshall Fields in Chicago, insisted that he try to secure a patent.

Lowell applied for a patent on May 5, 1922. He received his patent for a wood insertion tee (#1,493,687) on May 13, 1924

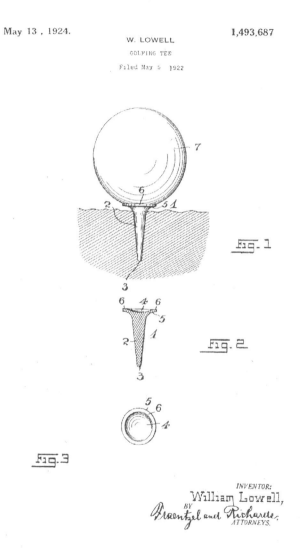

1924 – Dr. William Lowell, Sr. Wood Insertion Tee

Patented May 13, 1924

WILLIAM LOWELL – Patent 1,493,687

UNITED STATES PATENT OFFICE

William Lowell, of South Orange, New Jersey,

Assignor, By direct and MESNE Assignments, to the

NIEBLO M'F'G. CO. Inc, of Newark, N. Y.

A CORPORATION OF NEW JERSEY

<u>GOLFING TEE</u>

Application filed May 5, 1922 Serial No. 558,653

To all whom it may concern:

Be it known that I, WILLIAM LOWELL, a citizen of the United States, residing at South Orange, in the county of Essex and State of New Jersey, have invented certain new and useful Improvements in Golfing Tees; and I do hereby declare the following to be a full, clear, and exact description of the invention, such as will enable others skilled in the art to which it appertains to make and use the same, reference being had to the accompanying drawings, and to characters of reference marked thereon, which form a part of this specification.

This invention relates, generally, to improvements in that class of devices, known as tees for use upon the green of a golf course, and for the placing thereon of a golf-ball, the device being very simple in its construction and being easily forced into its

49

proper position upon the green, so as to be of immediate use, and to enable the player to dispense with the building up with wet sand of the usual tee.

The present invention, therefore, has for its principal object to prove a novel and simply constructed device of the character hereinafter more fully set forth, and to be used as a tee by golfers, the golfing tee being formed of a single piece of material comprising a cone-shaped shank having a pointed end so as to be readily forced into the ground, and having a disc-shaped member connected with and carried by said shank, said member being dished or concaved in its upper surface to conform to the surface of the golf-ball and being surrounded by a marginal ball-retaining and supporting rim, and said shank being centrally disposed with relation to the said ball supporting member.

The Principle purposes of the present invention is to provide a neat and cheap teeing device, which can be carried in the pockets of the player, the cost of production of the device being so slight, that the loss of an individual teeing device may be considered nil, and the device, if struck by the player may be readily replaced by another or; if not struck may be left in the green, another teeing device being used by the player upon the next green.

The device which is usually made of wood may also be made of the matter, which will disintegrate and will act in the manner of a fertilizer, if left in the green.

Another object of the present invention is to provide a device, such as is hereinafter more fully described, which will enable the player to dispense with the building up of a tee with wet sand and or dirt, thereby preventing any soiling of the hands, and doing away with the usual rubbing of the soiled hands upon the garments worn by the player.

Other objects of the present invention not at this time more particularly enumerated will be clearly understood from the following detailed description of the present invention.

With the various objects of the present invention in view, the said invention consists in the novel golfing tee hereinafter more fully set forth.

The invention is illustrated in the accompany drawings, in which: **Figure 1** is an elevation of a golfing tee made according to and embodying the principles of the present invention, the same being shown in its position, when its pointed shank is pushed or forced into the ground, and showing placed upon its dished or concaved supporting member, a golf ball ready to be struck by the player.

Figure 2 is a vertical sectional representation of the said golfing tee; and **Figure 3** is a top view of the same.

Similar characters of reference are employed in all of the said above described views, to indicate corresponding parts.

Referring now to the several figures of the drawing, he reference-character **1** indicates a complete golfing tee made according to and embodying the principles of the present invention, the same comprising a main body-member of a shank **2,** preferably cone-shaped as here shown, although this is not essential, and tapering at one end in a driving point, as **3,** for readily forcing or pressing the shank into the ground. Connected with the opposite end-portion of said body member **4**, which is dished –out or concaved in its upper surface, as at **5,** conforming to the surface of the golf ball, and which is surrounded by the marginal rim, as 6, all for the mounting and properly placing upon said disk-shaped portion or member **4**, of a golf-ball **7**, thereon, when the device has been pushed or pressed into the ground, as will be clearly evident from an inspection of said **Figure 1** of the drawings.

The said golfing tee herein-above described is usually made of wood, in any suitable manner, by turning or otherwise, or the same may be pressed into the desired shape by means of suitable molds, any suitable material, such as celluloid, rubber, or the like being used; and, if desired, a vegetable material may be used, which disintegrates when left in the ground, and may be used as a fertilizer.

The device itself is usually made much smaller than shown in the accompany drawings, and being very cheaply made and hence, costing but very little may be used in a profligate manner, the used tee, after having driven the golf ball, being left in the ground, and another golfing tee being used for the next drive of the ball.

With a golfing tee of the character hereinbefore described it will be evident that every part of the supporting cup or dished ball receiving member is in contact with the surface of the golf ball, and consequently the golfing tee is made in such a manner as to support the golf ball with a small or minimum contact with the same, and it is due to this small contact with the surface of the golf ball that there is no resistance to the flight of the ball when the same is struck with the golf club; and, furthermore, when certain kinds of strokes are made there can be no objectionable "back-spin" of the ball.

Furthermore, the hereinbefore described golfing tee provides a supporting medium or a very small size, thus making it impossible when using a tee, to have the face of the club come in contact with the tee after the ball surface has been struck and the ball sent upon its way.

I claim:

A golfing tee, formed of a single piece of material comprising a cone-shaped shank having a pointed end so as to be readily pressed into the ground, and a disk-shaped member connected with and carried by said shank, said member being dished or concaved in its upper surface to conform to the surface of the ball and surrounding by a marginal ball-retaining and supporting rim, said shank being centrally disposed with relation to the said dished ball-supporting member.

In testimony, that I claim the invention set forth above I have hereunto set my hand this 3rd day of May, 1922.

Witnesses:

Fredk. C. Fraentzel

Eva E. Densch

Lowell applied for another patent on August 25, 1925. He received his patent for a surface tee (#1.650,141) on Nov. 22, 1927.

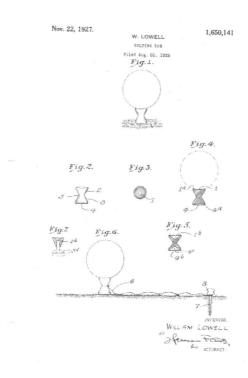

1927 – William Lowell Surface Tee

Lowell applied for another patent on Dec. 7, 1925. He received his patent for a gutta-percha topped tee (#1,670,627) May 22, 1928.

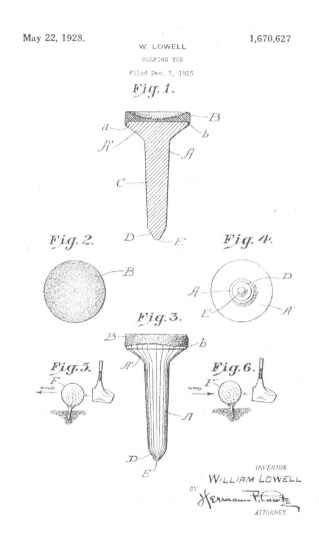

1925 – William Lowell Gutta-percha Top Insertion Tee

Lowell also applied for a patent on Nov. 13, 1925. He received his patent for an adjustable putter (#1,569,765) on Jan. 12, 1926

The gutta-percha tee became the first successfully marketed plastic tee, but it was short lived because it proved brittle.

Dr. Lowell's golf tee genius and thought process included the concepts of limiting mower problems; biodegradable potential; ease of carrying; design elements that eliminated golf club impact; ease of insertion; stable platform for a ball in windy condition; color; cost, value and safety.

Lowell had 5,000 prototype tees produced prior to receiving his first patent. He painted them green so that the tee would not look littered. He expected the Maplewood members would discard them after one use and thus packaged 18 of them in one small box. The members like the tees but did not like the green color because they wanted to use them again; they were difficult to find in the grass. So Lowell painted them red and called them the "Reddy Tee". Lowell's sons formed a company called Nieblo Manufacturing Corporation; the person who supplied the venture capital was Walter Niebling, a wealthy Newark commercial landowner who, coincidentally, was married to Lowell's daughter, Isabel.

Celebrity Endorsement

The Lowell's went to work trying to market the tees. The first results were poor – even though William Jr. had an obvious inside track at Marshal Fields. Lowell chose wood for the material because that was the least expensive way to get 5,000 prototype tees produced. The *"real thing"* was made of hardwood so that they would be durable. The Nieblo Manufacturing Corp. contracted an initial order of 50,000 tees made of white birch from the Novelty Turning Mill based in Norway, Maine.

The marketing plan was to advertise heavily. The initial advertising budget was $385. A box of 18 Reddy Tees cost 25 cents. The Lowell brothers split their territories, Ernest pounding around clubs and courses in the New York Metropolitan area and William Jr. working around the Chicago area where golf was growing quickly.

Major sports and department stores were not initially interested in the Reddy Tee. Club professionals were not keen either. The professionals were not sure that the tee were legal; sand was still in vogue and the Reddy Tee was yet another tee invention that promised to be gone soon – just like all the other tee inventions. The Lowell brothers were banging their heads against the wall and thus decided to change marketing strategy. The strategy they would ultimately use, chose them.

William Jr. met Jock Hutchinson, the well-known British golfer who had won the PGA Championship and the Open Championship. Lowell showed Hutchinson the Reddy Tee, but then produced some from his own pocket, delighted that he could find replacements. More importantly, Hutchinson sent Lowell to Doug Tweedy, the general manager of Spalding's Chicago store. *"Tell him I want the tees in all their stores."*

Good things were also happening in Manhattan where Nieblo had just opened an office on 23rd Street. One day, Walter Hagen (the most successful and famous professional of the time) and well-known trick shot artist Joe Kirkwood came to the office to get some Reddy Tees. (Dr. Lowell's granddaughter said that the event may have taken place at Dr. Lowell's dental office in Maplewood.)

His stock of Reddy Tees now replenished, Hagen started sticking the tee behind his ear and other professionals soon wanted what Hagen was using. Nieblo paid Hagen a significant endorsement fee of $1,500, and even produced tees with Hagen's signature on top. Young children, when watching the professionals play, would often scramble to collect one of the tees after the golfer had used it. This led to some courses roping off teeing areas as the children sometimes got too close to the players and there were worries about injuries.

Walter Hagen won 45 PGA tournaments including 11 majors. The Masters had not yet been played. He won the U.S. Open in 1914 and 1919; He won the British Open in 1922, 1924, 1928 & 1929; He won the PGA in 1921, 1924, 1925, 1926 & 1927; and he was captain of the first six Ryder Cups

Joe Kirkwood was the first Australian to win a PGA tournament, the 1923 Houston Invitational. He had 16 professional wins and 13 PGA wins. He won the Australian Open and the New Zealand Open in 1920; He won the Canadian Open in 1933. During his lifetime he had 29 one-in-ones, two in the same round. In 1924 he toured with Hagen as a trick shot artist.

The market was clearly accepting the Reddy Tee. Walter Hagen was on board. Spalding was selling the tees in its retail operations. And course professionals were buying the tees as well. Dr. Lowell's version of the insertion tee was revolutionizing the game; the boxes holding sand and water were disappearing.

The Nieblo Manufacturing Company, after some lean years, started to flourish financially. Revenues in 1929 were $165,000. In 2007 dollars, this was well over $2.5 million.

The company continued to advertise aggressively, producing one of the first 4-color advertisements in advertising history. They also sponsored professional golf tournaments including one at Winged Foot where professionals played for *"a whopping $5,000 purse"*. In 1929, the company's advertising budget was $27,000.

There is no official record at that time of whether or not Nieblo hired an advertising agency but work would indicate they did. However, it is clear that the Lowell boys took their advertising extremely seriously, but also had fun with it. One of the Reddy Tee advertisements features a cartoon of an unhappy golfer getting mud all over him hitting a tee shot. Next to him was a clean happy golfer using a ball teed on a "Reddy Tee".

A box of *"Reddy Tees"* reads…

"Little Tommy Niblick"

Built on a tee of sand,

Getting dirt upon his clothes

As well as on his hand.

Now he's learned to play the game

Clean as clean can be.

He drives'em far, and fair and true,

Thanks to "Reddy Tee"

Get'em from any "Pro" or Golf Shop or

Send us a 2 Cent stamp for a trial box.

Dr. Lowell's sons had proven to their father that the tee could be a financial success – at least initially.

Then the lawyers got involved.

Competitors and Imitators

Dr. Lowell secured another patent in 1928, best described as an attempt to improve his original design, using a gutta-percha top. The design, however, ultimately proved too brittle.

As sales of the Reddy Tee took off, competitors moved in. The 1928 patent was an attempt to "take on" what Dr. Lowell deemed as "imitators and thieves"; it did nothing to scare them off. Despite advice from his sons, Lowell was determined to sue competitors, eventually spending $140,000 on infringement suits. Other companies were manufacturing golf tees from different materials and altering the design slightly – or at least enough to make them legal.

In 1929, in the New York Court of Appeals, Judge Learned Hand stated, *"Dr. Lowell was unquestionably the inventor of the golf tee."* But, Hand also pointed out that his patent did not protect the invention sufficiently. This was bad news for Lowell and the Nieblo Manufacturing Company: their monopoly was over and they had spent most of their profits on legal fees.

In 1933, in the middle of the Great Depression, the Company was insolvent. Lawyers advised Dr. Lowell and his sons to declare bankruptcy. However, with a great deal of pride (and a big inventory) Dr. Lowell decided to repay all creditors. Looking back, with the benefit of hindsight, Dr. Lowell probably would have been better off had he sold the company when it was at its most profitable point. And it's likely that he would have enjoyed more profits longer if he had spent the money on advertising and promotion instead of litigation. Dr. Lowell's decision to fight those who were infringing on his patent perhaps makes more sense in the context of the competitive arena at the time. The register of golf tee patents from 1921 – 1930 shows that the U.S. Patent Office granted 136 patents for tees.

Approved devices included insertion tees, sand molds, rubber tees, paper tees, tethered tees, wires, pegs, pins, metal tees, and even a pencil tee from G. H. Eddy of Foster Washington and a spring loaded dispenser from A. E. Buhrke of River Forest, Illinois.

The United States Patent Office grants patent for either Utility or Design patents. They are also given to plants. A patent gives its owner the right to exclude others from making, using and selling the patented invention. To receive a patent, an invention must meet three criteria.

Useful: Virtually any usefulness will suffice, provided that it is functional and not aesthetic.

Novel: It must differ physically in some way from all prior art. The physical hardware must be different, there must be a new combination of hardware, or there must be a new one.

Non-obvious: The differences between you invention and prior art must not be obvious to one with ordinary skill in the field.

Utility Patent

A utility patent protects functional aspects of an invention and, once issued, usually last for 20 years from its filing date.

Design Patent

A design patent protects the decorative aspects of an invention for a term of 14 years. Design patents should be pursued if the essence of an invention is its appearance, or if the final version has a unique look.

Both types of patents give an exclusive right for the holder of the patent to manufacture, license and sell the product.

Each patent application must have a title for the product. These vary significantly but prove some insight into the mind of the inventor.

Examples of Golf Tee and related inventions:

Means for forming tees for golf tees

Directional Golf Tee

Golf Teeing Machine

Golf Tee Positioning Device

Molded Object

Golf Tee Magazine

Articulated Tee

Tee Off Apron

Flexible Golf Tee

Combined Swing and Line Indicator

Tee Setting Device

Golf Tee Dibble

Tee Handling Device

Swizzle Stick

Tee Driving Means

Golf Tee Leveling and Driving Instrument

Tilt-top Golf Tee

Gauge for Placing Tee

Turf Inserting Part

Tee Setting Accessory for a Golf Show

Tee Positioning Device

High Performance Golf Tee

Heads Down Golf Practice Device

Tee Off Device

Golf Tool

Biodegradable Tees

Paper Tees

Cigarette and Cigar Holder

GOLF Tee Awl

Golf Tee Insertion Device

Line of Flight Indicator

Golf Tee Holder

Golfing Aid

Flanged Golf Tee Collar

Placement Device for Tee & Ball

Tilt-top Golf Tee

Tee Holding Device

Adjustable Golf Tee

Device for Retrieval

Golf Tee with Rotatable Head

Practice Golf Tee

Aiming Aid for Tee

Golf Tee Manufacturing Method

Grappling Device

Golf Club Face Cleaning Tool

Offset Golf Tee

Anchored Golf Tee

Calibrated Golf Tee

Tee Sight

Back-swing Training Device

Pilot Hole Drill for Golf Tee

Golf Tee Stand

Ground Anchoring Mechanism

Golf Tee Inserter

Adjustable Height Golf Tee

Golf Tee Inserting Height gauge

Golf Tee with Crown Shaped Head

Coupled Golf Tees

Golf Ball Holder

Brush Tee

Impact Boosting Power Tee

Golf Tee Marking System

Golf Ball Support

Writable Golf Tee

CHAPTER V

The *"Classic"* Lowell Tee Design

THE "LOWELL" WOODEN TEE

There is much more to placing a ball on a tee than just swinging. To maximize the result of any golf shot using a tee, the golfer should have as much golf tee and club related product knowledge as possible. He must know his or her personal club head speed; He must understand the length and stiffness of his clubs shaft… He must understand his ball – construction, compression and spin rates; He must know and understand his clubs and the distances and launch angles he can achieve with each driver, fairway wood, hybrid, iron, or wedge; He must understand his ball striking ability; Then he must apply the equipment's combined benefits with a golf tee at the right height to maximize his results.

Each round of golf offers 18 opportunities to put your ball on a tee. The tee will allow for the cleanest strike of the ball and should always be used.

Criteria for Evaluation

Recent new technology in the manufacture of clubs, balls and shafts has revolutionized the golfing business and requires a complete understanding of the teed height of each tee shot.

Design must follow function. The height of the ball on the tee must be exact to the vertical center of the club to hit the *"sweet spot"* consistently to standardize the distance of each shot. That understanding must factor in the elements of nature; course elevation, humidity, the wind and most importantly the ball. Understanding launch angle and the center of gravity design elements of clubs are essential to successful and creative shot making.

Since there is only one small definite *"sweet spot"* on any hitting surface, hitting the ball squarely and consistently will achieve the desired results.

Design Fundamentals of the "Classic" Lowell Golf Tee

The May 13, 1924 William Lowell Sr. Golf Tee patent #1,493,687 has all the fundamental elements that have proven to be the standard for insertion tees.

"A golf tee, formed of a single piece of material comprising of a cone-shaped shank having a pointed end so as to be readily pressed into the ground, and a disc-shaped member connected

with and carried by said shank, said member being dished or concaved in its upper surface to conform to the surface of the ball and surrounded by a marginal ball-retaining and supporting rim, said shank being centrally disposed with relation to said dished ball-supporting member."

Additionally, on May 22, 1928 Dr. Lowell received a second Golf Tee patent #1,670,627 that featured a gutta-percha top. The tee was to support a later version of the Reddy Tee that consisted of a celluloid top and wooden shaft and manufactured in Canada.

Following are the claims of the 1928 patent:

"A golf tee comprising a stem having a tapering point at one end and an enlarged portion at the other end, a head formed of relatively non-chipping material at the upper end and having a cupped upper surface with a peripheral ball-supporting rim, and downwardly extending peripheral sides on the head and stem being axially united to form a unit article with head rigidly supported when the stem is pressed into the ground."

Elements & Considerations for the Classic Lowell Insertion Golf Tee

1) *Available for immediate use.*
2) *Easily carried in the pocket, preferably with a medium point so as to not stick through the clothing.*
3) *Very simple, neat and cheap in construction, so as to be inexpensive. (Wood to be turned or pressed. Plastic, celluloid, rubber or the like, to be molded or injection molded. So inexpensive, as to be left in the ground, discarded or reused if desired).*

4) *So light in weight that a stroke with a golf club would not drive the tee in any way to endanger anyone by impact. So light that the tee would have no objectionable characteristics when left in the ground, with lawn mowers or otherwise.*

5) *A single piece of material, usually wood that is biodegradable. This could also be plastic or biodegradable material which will disintegrate and could be fertilizer.*

6) *A cone-shaped shank, having a pointed end so as to be readily forced into the ground. In varied lengths, the shank allows for exacting depths or insertion into the ground.*

7) *Small dished-out, concave or points in its upper portion surface that nest the outer surface of the golf ball, surrounded by marginal ball-retaining and supporting rim. An upper portion surface that offers minimal resistance to the flight of the ball and impossible to come into contact with the golf club until the ball is well on its way.*

8) *Invisible when addressing the ball.*

On November 22, 1927 William Lowell Sr. received yet another Golf Tee patent #1,650,141. This invention was a **surface tee** that appears to be an attempt to widen the Nieblo product line of golf tee choices. It is not known if this product was ever manufactured.

"A golf tee comprising a double-ended reversible wooden support for a golf ball of a maximum diameter less than one third of the diameter of the golf ball, both ends of the support being recessed so that either end may serve as a base and other as a rest for the ball, the rims of the recessed ends being serrations into the surface thereof, said ends being joined by a constricted body

portion, a ground-penetrating peg having an enlarged distinctively visible head, and a flexible connection attached at one end to the constricted body portion of the tee and at the other end of a peg, the head of said peg being formed with a constricted portion whereby the peg may be readily extracted from the ground."

On Jan. 12, 1926 Dr. William Lowell Sr. also received patent #1,569,765 for an <u>adjustable length of golf club</u> having a slide able, rotatable grip. There is no mention that it was ever produced.

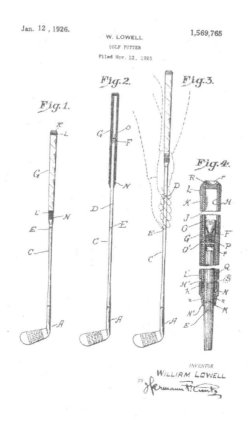

"An adjustable length of golf club having a slide able rotatable grip, a shaft having a rigidly attached head at one end and a substantial portion of the other end of the shaft fitting loosely within the grip, a tight sliding bearing adjacent the end of the shaft engaging a small area of contact inside the grip, and a readily releasable clamping surface at the inner end of the grip, whereby the grip may be readily shifted longitudinally to any position on the shaft within a predetermined range, and may within range of movement be rigidly united with the shaft, and an exterior means on the grip to effect such union."

In 1943, the Lowell's sold the company to Red Devil Tool for $10,000. The patents had run out and the Spaulding and Wilson companies were producing and selling millions of tees under their own brand names. Dr. William Lowell Sr. died in 1954 at the age of 91. His original design has stood the test of time and today everyone recognizes and uses the "Classic" Lowell Wood Tee Design and design criteria.

CHAPTER VI

The "Lowell" Family

By Joan Lowell Smith

Joan Lowell Smith (daughter of William Lowell Jr.) is a multiple award-winning newspaper reporter and syndicated columnist who has written the weekly pet column since 1996 for New Jersey's largest daily newspaper, The Star-Ledger. This is her personal story about how her family invented and marketed the Reddy Tee.)

Dr. William Lowell Sr. & William Lowell Jr.

73

My grandfather, William Lowell Sr., was a formidable figure. Anything he tackled had to be the best whether it involved music, sports or dentistry. He seldom failed at anything he attempted with the possible exception of me as a violin student. A concert violinist with the Hayden String Quartet, his attempts to transform me into an overnight violin virtuoso at age eight failed abysmally. I'm convinced that brand of impatience with imperfection in himself and others is what led to invention of the golf tee.

Grandfather also sang baritone solos at the Riverside Presbyterian Church in New York City. How he managed the talent to excel while maintaining a thriving dental practice in South Orange, New Jersey, remains an unsolved mystery.

Neatness Counts

An athlete too, he played a mean game of tennis at Orange Lawn Tennis Club in West Orange until he hit 60 when his game failed to mirror his expectations of perfection. Switching to the less physically taxing game of golf, he joined Maplewood Country Club in 1921. While he took to the game quickly, because he was fastidious to a fault and balked at groveling in wet sand to form a mound to tee-up the ball, a totally repugnant practice going back to the very beginning of the game hundreds of years before. No way would he tolerate abrasions to his delicate fingers nor soil his pristine plus-fours.

A man of action, he resolved the filthy practice by employing his own ingenuity. With no altruistic thoughts whatsoever, he fashioned the first golf tee with his own adept hands, refusing to subject himself to wet sand piles a moment longer.

Many golf writers claimed his first tee was whittled from a flagpole. Close enough. My dad, William Lowell, Jr., who maintained assiduous journals on every aspect of golf tee history, said his dad actually whittled the original tee from the stick of a small parade flag. (Grandfather had initiated the first Fourth of July parade in Maplewood and had plenty of flags around.)

The origin of the messy mounds was described well in an article from the March 3, 2003 issue of The New Yorker magazine: "William Lowell Sr., a dentist from Maplewood, New Jersey, extracted from a wooden dowel the shape familiar now and called it the Reddy Tee... For five or six hundred years (in Scotland), golfers teed up their balls on handfuls of loose sand. After completing a hole, they reached into the hole itself and picked up some sand. The rules instructed them to do that and to set up their little piles within two club-lengths of the hole and tee off for the next one. Teeing grounds and putting surfaces were not separated until late in the nineteenth century.

The First Round

Grandfather tracked down a wood turner to produce the first – and only – order of 5,000 green tees replicating his prototype. Dad and his older brother Ernest, both salesmen, instantly grasped the merchandising potential of the tee and pushed their father to obtain a patent. Initially grandfather was apathetic, perfectly happy to keep the tees for his own personal use.

Besides, other golfers made fun of his invention, bombarding him with the questions: *"Why should anyone pay for wooden tees when the sand is free?"*

When grandfather invented the tee, dad was working in Chicago as a sporting good buyer at Marshall Field. Already hooked on golf, he maximized his selling techniques playing every club worth its salt in the area where he would corner pros to convince them to carry tees in their pro shops. To broaden the sales campaign, from his journal, he wrote: *"(In 1926) made several researches through the use of questionnaires to golf clubs throughout the country. Over 2,000 letters brought in over 700 replies which put us in a better position to determine merchandising."*

Significant financial backing from wealthy Walter Niebling, married to grandfather's oldest daughter Isabel, enabled the Nieblo Company (contraction of Niebling and Lowell) to open offices in New York on 23rd Street in 1922. The corporate name changed to The Reddy Tee Company once the patent and trademark were issued in 1924.

Star Support

The tee was a hard sell until dad met Jock Hutchinson, 1921 PGA champ who, like most tour pros, had already received samples of tees, 18 to a box. From dad's journal: Jock was excited and asked me, *"Please tell me where can I get more of these?"*

Almost simultaneously another super star, Walter Hagen, arrived by limousine at grandfather's dental practice in South Orange accompanied by Joe Kirkwood, golf trick star, asking basically the same question. Hutchinson, Hagen and Kirkwood sealed the deal when they turned their backs on sandboxes and switched to Reddy Tees. By 1922 when it was Hagen's turn to win the PGA title, he was driving off Reddy Tees and would stash one over an ear.

In *"The Walter Hagen Story, by The Haig, Himself"* (1956, Simon and Schuster) Hagen wrote: "For over 400 years golfers had pinched a bit of sand into a suitable tee for their drives. There had been no artificial change in the practice since the game's origin. In 1921 Dr. William Lowell, a New Jersey dentist, a novice golfer with no great respect for the revered traditions of the game, whittled out a little wooden peg on which to mount his ball for the drive. Playing companions ridiculed the idea, but his sons induced the doctor to patent the gadget and put it on the market. The little peg thus manufactured, painted red, was advertised to the golf world as the Reddy Tee. Professional golfers dismissed it as silly and refused to accept the tees as gifts. Amateurs shrugged off their use. Even the ladies of the game looked down their pretty noses at Dr. Lowell's little invention. Hagen was quoted… *"Probably nothing would have come of the tee had not Joe Kirkwood and I decided to use them as a sort of added attraction on our exhibition tour of 1922."* That, and the fact that the good doctor shelled out $1,500 as a persuader. (All true.)

As other pros began using Reddy Tees in tournaments, spectators would rush to grab the pros' discarded tees and soon clamored for their own supplies. A box of 18 tees sold for 25 cents, a tidy sum in those days compared to sand which was free.

Still, sale skyrocketed. Initially tees were only available in pro shops, but public demand persuaded the family to branch out to Macys, Bambergers and Abercrombie and Fitch.

Tee Party

By 1932, factories were producing million of tees made from the finest white birch in Norway, Maine (first factory), Orchard, Massachusetts; Brantford, Canada and England with a customer base stretching to Mexico, Great Britain, Central and South American, Alaska, Hawaii, the Philippines, Bermuda and West Indies.

No one was more surprised at the acceptance of the tee than grandfather who continued to practice dentistry while his sons ran the business with a small office staff. By this time dad had deserted Chicago to become vice president, settling in Maplewood a couple miles from the country club.

Tournament Sponsor

In 1927 the company staged a golf tournament. As dad told it. *"(We) Held the first one at Green Brook Country Club in Caldwell, New Jersey with a record field of 169 entries, among them two national champions (he didn't say which ones). Publicity alone resulting from this tournament far exceeded the cost and inestimable goodwill."*

Quite unintentionally, the company also made a significant contribution to advertising history. Lavish sums were spent on advertising resulting in one of the first ever four-color ads. A member of Maplewood Country Club who taught advertising at

Rutgers University said he used a Reddy Tee in his classes as a prime example of early full color ads. One ad from 1929 in my collection could challenge today's best ad copy. Another promoted a tournament in June 1929 at Winged Foot Golf Club, Mamaroneck, New York, sponsored by the Reddy Tee Company offering a "Whopping" $5,000 purse.

Sales figures show the company's stellar year was 1929, year of the Great Depression. Profits soared to $165,256. Converted to today's dollars it would be in the millions. Profits would have been higher except for the enormous advertising budget which was $27,000 in 1929 alone.

Competitors Surface

Although the Lowell patent was not the first for a teeing device, more importantly it was the first and only tee manufactured and accepted by the golfing public. Other patents were granted in England for teeing devices and George Grant, also a dentist, issued one in Massachusetts in 1899. While Grant made enough tees to distribute to friends and family, he never manufactured them. Golfers worldwide continued to form messy sand mounds until grandfather's invention wiped out the grimy practice for good.

As sales soared, despite advice from his sons, grandfather's pride and feisty temper emerged when competitors appeared in droves. (Didn't I say he was formidable?). In 1925 he filed another patent granted in 1928 clarifying what the tee did and did not do. For example, he mentioned that his tee was *"so light in weight that a stroke with golf club would not drive the article in a way to endanger anyone by impact"*, and went on to specify other minutia. Despite all the specificity, the new patent did nothing to scare away competitors.

Determined to sue all pretenders, he squandered $140,000 in infringement suits. He took one suit to the New York Court of Appeals in 1929, where the esteemed Judge Learned Hand stated: *"Dr. Lowell was unquestionably the inventor of the golf tee"*, but that his patent did not protect his invention sufficiently. Companies were manufacturing tees from different materials and altering them slightly from those pictured in the patent art.

Grandfather's patents may not have been ironclad but he was ahead of his time with the inclusion of a clause in the original patent for biodegradable tees. Frustrated that he could not create the perfect formula to accomplish that air, he *"settled"* for wood. But still his unattainable goal of a tee that would disintegrate led him to select green for his first order of 5,000 wooden tees, his assumption being that the golfer would hit the ball, move on to his second shot and leave the tee behind. Wrong. Instead, golfers willing to try the new fangled wooden peg wisely saved tee that didn't break. The color was quickly switched to red, inspiring the trademark and corporate name: *"The Reddy Tee"*. They were *"ready"* and they were red. Soon tees were produced in any bright color of the spectrum – other than green.

Getting it right

In 1962 one of golfdom's most prominent and prolific writers, Charlie Price, wrote *"The World of Golf"*, a voluminous book published by Random House. When dad was upset by an error on tee history, I offered to write to Price who had said in his book: *"In the second year of business with The Reddy Tee Company, Lowell grossed more than $300,000, largely on one order from F. W. Woolworth & Co. for a billion tees."* Dad went ballistic. From his journal: *"We had repeatedly refused to sell to Woolworth. Upon being refused a selling arrangement with us, they bought from another manufacturer in Vermont run by the Bump brothers."* The Reddy Tee Company lost that suit.

Because I was a legal secretary on Wall Street at that time, I knew enough legal lingo that my letter gave Price the erroneous impression that I was a lawyer. It also earned a lunch with him at Toots Shor's restaurant in the city. He promised to correct his minor error in the future book – which he did – and we became good friends.

As a result of that connection dad turned over all data on the tee to me, proclaiming me official *"family golf tee historian"*. Besides his journals, his voluminous collection included ledgers, ads, books and articles going back to the twenties plus precious letter from Bobby Jones and other luminaries. In one, Jones wrote, *"We should all be grateful to your father for inventing the Reddy Tee."* Of all the top golfers dad knew in the 20s and 30s his favorites were Jones, Hagen, Bryan Nelson, Sam Snead, the Demaret brothers and Craig Wood. He was also fond of golf writers Grantland Rice, Red Hoffman, Sid Dorfman – and eventually Price.

Family Passion

Not surprisingly, golf was always important in our home. Dad lived for the game. In his best years he shot in the low 80s and occasionally the high 70s. He was still playing six months before he died in 1976 at 79. Mom won a tournament at Maplewood. My older brother Bill still shoots in the 80s. Dad taught me to play when I was 13. Because we spend countless hours at the driving range before he'd let me out on the course, I became sensational off the tee (!) but the closer I got to the magic hole my game would disintegrate. If I could hire a pro to putt for me we could join the tour in tandem.

In my youth, I seldom mentioned grandfather's invention to friends assuming no one would care. But one day while sipping sodas at a local fountain with a friend I bragged a bit. Big mistake! When I announced that my grandfather had invented the golf tee, she showed more interest in her soda. Two boys sitting next to her, however, were glued to the exchange. One piped up: *"And my grandfather ownes the Brooklyn Bridge."* *"Really?"* was my stunned reply. I believed him. Obviously, he didn't believe me.

In 1954 dad took me to the U.S. Open at Baltusrol Golf Club in Springfield, New Jersey, 11 years after he had sold the Company to Red Devil Tool for a paltry $10,000. By that time the patents had run out and Spalding and Wilson were producing tees in the billions.

That day at Baltusrol, we were strolling along a fairway when Jimmy Demaret approached. "Hi ya, Bill," he yelled as though he'd seen him the week before. Craig Wood, there as a spectator, greeted him similarly. The day became especially memorable when Craig introduced us to the "new generation" of golfers in the competition – Mike Souchak, Dick Mayer, Roberto DiVincenzo and Jerry Barber.

After the demise of The Reddy Tee Company, dad became a salesman for Union Bag and Paper Company where the inventive gene emerged. He designed the original six-pack for Krueger Beer and the heat-sealed bag during World War II. He didn't make a fortune since he had to sign away patent rights, but they did toss a testimonial dinner for him and awarded him an engraved silver cup.

Recognition

Maplewood Country Club invited me to a gala dinner in 1986 to celebrate the installation of a bronze plaque in the lobby commemorating the invention of the tee, emblazoned *"Birthplace of the Tee"*, grandfather's name and patent number. Since then, their golf season begins with the annual *"Dr. Lowell Memorial Golf Tournament"*. To my utter embarrassment, when I was asked to launch the first tournament using one of the original short tees, I managed to shank it into a nearby creek. I wanted to follow the ball into the creek after my ignominious flub, unfortunately captured by a television crew.

Another honor was bestowed in 1998 when grandfather was inducted into the New Jersey Inventors Hall of Fame for his invention which I accepted on behalf of the family.

Reddy Tee exhibits are on display in the Golf House Museum at USGA Headquarters in Far Hills, New Jersey and the PGA Museum in Ponte Vedra, Florida. Dad donated two of the last remaining original tee to each museum in 1974. I have the other one.

Almost 40 years after dad took me to Baltusrol; my husband Warren entered the pro-am event preceding the 1992 Buick Classic at Westchester Country Club, Harrison New York. Warren was paired with Ben Crenshaw, as soon as he said that his wife's grandfather invented the golf tee. Ben – known as a premier golf historian – responded without missing a beat: "Oh sure, Dr. Lowell!"

In the August 29, 1999 daily edition of The Star –Ledger based in Newark, New Jersey, Amy Nutt wrote an article devoted to "New Jersey Firsts", a book by Tom Wilk and Harry Armstrong. The authors celebrated every New Jersey invention from Teflon to Band-Aids, air conditioners, tranquilizers and the first condensed soup (Campbell's), not to mention Edison's triumphs. Nutt quoted Armstrong: *"I love the golf tee! There are so many technical firsts in our book and golf tee is just this little piece of wood.*

It's so simple and so obvious and yet nobody thought of it until William Lowell Sr. did."

Joan Lowell Smith Side Bars from conversations:

Ken: I groaned at the long list of questions and didn't have a chance until now to get to them. Initially on 5/25 you said you wanted me "to write anything and everything you feel important about your family's efforts to market the first successful golf tee. Include as much as you want. I thought I did that. Evidently I didn't go far enough.

First - I'll address your questions in order before I give you some detailed tidbits you should like:

There are no original prototypes as I said earlier.

I know of no formal collections other than the two premier museums. Maybe Irv Valenta knows of others.

I have no info on companies that produced "different tees" and don't know exactly what you mean. The Reddy Tee Company produced celluloid, two-part tees, different sizes and colors at factory locations mentioned.

There was no contract other than a handshake with Hagen and Kirkwood when the $1,500 check was presented. To my knowledge nothing was paid to Hutchinson. Ton of articles and books refer to Hagen and Kirkwood's early use of the tee. I only gave you a small selection of articles and quote from books but have much more.

I have no photos of early pros using tees.

I mentioned the imprinted Hagen tees with his signature in my chapter. The one I have is very valuable and I wouldn't let it out of my hands nor any of the other tees. Aren't you coming here at some point? You're welcome to take plenty of pix. I have a spectrum of tees of various shapes, materials and colors. The green one has turned so dark over the years, I'm afraid it would look almost black except with a terrific camera.

In addition to the 4-color ad and the sign for the tournament referred to in my copy, I have price sheets and ads used in pro shops. When you have a publisher nailed down I'll make Xeroxes of those ads and the letters from Bobby Jones, Al Smith and Ben Crenshaw.

Don't know what you mean by "demonstration photos"?

I have no letters to or from patent attorneys. What do you mean by "original patents"?

I have some old B&W pix of the birch tree area in Norway, Maine. They'd have to be restored which shouldn't be too difficult.

I gave you profits of the best year rather than go through each year which could be boring reading but I have a simple ledger sheet of profits and advertising expenditures if you need it.

I'm not sure when the name was changed from Nieblo to The Reddy Tee Company, but it had to be between 1930 and 32. I have letter form 1930 on Nieblo letterhead and 1932 on The Reddy Tee Company letterhead.

Red Devil Tool is still in business selling tools. The owner back then, George Lee, was a friend of the family. He thought he'd produce tees but never did.

I have no copies of the 1926 questionnaire.

I have one original box of tees. Again, photos may be taken.

In my chapter I wrote that Hagen used a Reddy Tee when he won the PGA in 1922.

I have no info on where all the exhibitions were held, only the quoted reference from dad's journal.

I have no figures on gross sales. The reference to the "billions" produced by Spalding and Wilson is from dad's journal.

You'll like this from dad's journal on how he "landed" Spalding: "Jock asked why Spalding did not have the 'wonderful tees' and I told him how they had turned me down saying they didn't believe they'd sell. Jock said, "Go see Doug Tweedy, general manager at Spalding (in Chicago) and tell him I want him to put the wooden tees in ALL Spalding stores." Those were the magic words. Spalding listened. Monday morning I saw Tweedy and delivered Jock's message. He gave me an order for 30 dozen packages of 18 tees each.

Here goes with more details from dad's journal that you may want to insert wherever they fit, beginning with dad's move to

NJ in April 1925 to take over the business. (His brother Ernie only worked part time.)

"I selected the Novelty Turning Co. in Norway, Maine, one of the oldest in the woodturning business. The Brown family had owned and run it for four generations with a reputation for quality and reliability. After settling on terms I gave them a five-year contract. This arrangement turned out just fine – better tees and at a lower cost and dependable deliveries."

"We did business with Novelty from 1925 to 1943 when we sold. In 1925 with the tee production and other supplies arranged for on a firm basis, I now turned attention to advertising. Orders were increasing and so was competition. The first one – the Morley yellow tee – cut into our sales heavily as at that time we only had red and sales ran about 50/50."

"I started reviewing advertising agencies. The one we had wasn't cooperating. Out of 20 agencies interviewed I picked Erwin Wasey & Co., at one time one of the largest. The reason we got together was two-fold; their officers were golfers and were intrigued with this new innovation in golf and waived their usual retainer applied to accounts under $50,000 a year. For our part we appreciated the value of their enthusiasm. The arrangement worked grand as we got a lot of free follow-up and research from some 20,000 newspapers even though our ads were just a few lines on Fridays. Because Wasey placed so much business with the papers we also came in on it as one of their clients. Years later I learned that his four-color ad for the tee have been used as examples of the tops in early four-color advertising. I know those ads contributed significantly to our success."

On the declining years:

After the stock market crash in October 1929 we held on for 3 ½ years by putting on a full line of golf equipment and selling to pros direct. We stayed in there by taking over Nibblet Fanders Co., a small distributor of golf supplies exclusively to the pros.

Even though the business trickled down to a $10,000 sale in 1943 no one can ever take away the fact that Dr. William Lowell was the inventor of the golf tee.

CHAPTER VII

The Brush-T *"Like driving a golf ball off fresh air."*

"It not only feels unlike any other golf tee before, it has been independently and scientifically proven to give longer and more accurate tee shots. It first appeared in South Africa in 1999, then gradually crept into the game in UK, USA and then into EU countries."

In 2003 at the South African Bureau of Standards (SABS) Design Awards Gala Dinner, Brush-T was given the prestigious award for its outstanding contribution to South African industrial design. According to one of the judging panelists, the Brush-T received one of the two unanimous top prizes. The SABS Design Institute has held its annual competition since 1969, aimed at stimulating excellence in industrial design and engineering. After much investment of time, money and political endorsement from the likes of Nelson Mandela and Thabo Mbeki, the scheme has grown immensely in stature over recent years – and the reasons are mainly economic. While gold, diamonds and tourism are synonymous with South Africa, the country vigorously courts overseas investment in its commerce and industry. South Africa design knowhow is definitely proven to be of world-standard, in areas diverse as advertising and mining.

In addition to the Award for Industrial Design, the Brush-T also won the prize for overall best product of the year – The Chairman's Award for Most Exceptional Entry.

COMPETITION BACKGROUND

The judging criteria were as follows:

Innovation

Cost/value relationship

Performance

Safety and ergonomics

Environmental impact

Ease of maintenance and installation

Quality of material used, manufacture and assembly

Appearance and tactile aspects

Marketing aspects

Trade potential

Brush-T allows you to drive your ball farther and more accurately. The unique qualities of the Brush-T means that the sidespin or interference, all too often associated with wooden tees can be eliminated. The bristles provide a raised support for the ball, but still give it unprecedented stability. Independent testing in San Diego, California using *"Iron Byron"* showed a marked improvement in the dispersion rate, delivering greater accuracy. Now, golfers can launch their drives without resistance or deflection and gain up to 7 additional yards.

The Brush-T is specifically engineered to compliment the size and launch angle of the larger oversized driver heads. The amazing longer revolutionary nylon bristles bend on impact reducing resistance associated with conventional wooden or plastic tees. Independent test prove less resistance produces dramatically longer and straighter drives.

The Brush-T took the 50th Annual PGA Show in Orlando by storm. Its' tougher material, bullet-like pod, belt clip and new colors resulted in distribution deals with new companies on all five continents and was suddenly a global brand.

Brush-T:

> Conforms to 2004 USGA and R&A rulings -

> Comes in four sizes to ensure consistent height for ideal launch angle and trajectory

> Care and Use instructions -

> Always store your Brush-T in its case to extend bristle life. When teeing up the ball, press the center of the top. Always push the Brush-T in the ground as far as it will go.

The story of the Brush-T
by Richard Crouse –Johannesburg Republic of South Africa

I am an avid golfer and the golfing-bug caught me fair and square in the seventies in London, England where my wife and I lived for eleven years. We both played whenever the opportunity arose. In the eighties we returned to South Africa where I opened a powder coating company. We were blessed with four children in England and another two in sunny South Africa.

I had started making my own four-ball as my eldest is a girl followed by five boys. My work allowed me to get to the driving range regularly and on the course twice a week.

In 1995 the idea of creating the perfect tee with the ball almost floating on air became a serious quest. After exploring the various plastic options, bristles became the only solution and I needed to make samples. This is no easy task and after asking my son Jason to assist me we both gave up and decided to get some professional help. I got in touch with the Taiwanese embassy and got a list of plastic injection factories with the capacity of bristling. I had explored every tooth-brush company in SA, but to no avail, as none were able to *"bristle"* small tees with long bristles. The Taiwanese factory was very helpful and they made us quite a few rough tees with bristles. These first Brush-T's were put to the test by me and they supported the ball adequately, but lacked the finesse of a real product.

I did enjoy the fact that they would last for months as opposed to minutes and they were especially economical on the driving range.

At this stage, the Taiwanese company quoted me a large amount of money to produce the tooling required for decent production runs. My business was taking a lot of my time and I temporarily put the Brush-T on hold before I could continue this dream.

My son Jason had just completed three years of Industrial Design College in Johannesburg and asked me whether he could continue work on my tee. I said that we had reached a stage that we needed a sponsor, so I would accompany him to a well known South African businessman and show him what we had achieved. The reaction we received was reversed. The fact that he knew nothing about golf may have been to our advantage, as he needed to ask for advice.

Jason put his experience to work and created some attractive packaging. We presented the new packaging to the sponsor and then he got excited. We had not fixed a name to our bristle tee so we asked our sponsor. He said that it was a *"Brush-T"* and so it came to be.

We had applied for patent protection and we were allowed to re-new the application after the first year. This is a saga on its own as there is no such thing as a *"world-wide patent"* and every part of the golfing world needs to be protected. An expensive and a time consuming exercise. All of this needed to be put in place before you can sell one tee. We were put in touch with a factory in China and Jason gave them all the drawings for the tees, the holder and the boxes.

We wrote to the Royal and Ancient and US PGA and submitted the Brush-T for their ruling to see whether it was legal or not. They gave us the thumbs up and the Brush-T was approved by both golfing bodies.

At this stage we were testing constantly. Our sample designs determined we would go with bristles stapled straight. The measurements between the bristles were crucial and we were satisfied the ball was getting the maximum support possible. We took the Brush-T to the windiest conditions South Africa coastal course had to offer and it was put through its paces. We enjoyed this testing period, but we had not experienced wet and humid conditions and we were to find out later that the bristles we choose failed to hold the ball adequately for eighteen holes under those conditions. We changed the bristles for the longer Brush-T's and overcame the problem.

We decided to test the Brush-T on the South African market and so we went to the largest golf retail outlet in the country. The buyer said No! He regarded the Brush-T as a gimmick and he was not prepared to stock it in his store. This was a problem because without their acceptance it would be difficult to develop credibility. We contacted one of the owners of this super-store and reminded him that he said that he would help us and stock the tee. The following day a very angry buyer called Jason and told him that he would take two hundred boxes. We supplied the order and were amazed that two days later he ordered five hundred boxes. Two days later he ordered another five hundred boxes, followed by two thousand followed by two thousand more. When the dust had cleared, we had sold seven-thousand Brush-T boxes in a three-week period. The buyer admits to this day, every time we meet, that he made the biggest mistake by not taking our product at the start. We now have a good relationship and they are our best and biggest outlet in SA.

Jason and I went to meet Ernie Els' manager to see what it would take to get the "Big Easy" to endorse our South African product. He gave us an important "in" to their golf club manufacturers testing facility in San Diego. Jason took the brush-T and went to American to do some vital tests. He had to make a special adaptation to their mechanical golfer so that it would accept the Brush-T. When it was all in place, they took readings to compare the findings under strict conditions between the Brush-T and a conventional wooden tee. The results were amazing as we could prove that the Brush-T was longer and straighter than the wooden tee and the reason was that the Brush-T had little or no resistance and little or no deflection. The ball actually leaves the Brush-T with less spin than the wooden tee and hence the reason for straighter and longer drives. The grouping of balls with the Brush-T, because of the reduced spin was very good and the advantage was between four and seven yards. Armed with these findings, we were ready to take Brush-T to other stores.

Through a series of contacts we were able to get Ernie Els to try Brush-T at St. Andrews in the last round of the Dunhill. Ernie shot a 65 and the commentators spoke about the Brush-T on the live broadcast. We had distributors clambering for our product and after an incredible golf expo in the south of England; we sold in excess of one hundred thousand boxes of Brush-Ts.

Golf shows followed in Japan and Australia and we began building a net-work of distributors in many countries. We had show the product at the PGA Golf Expo in Orlando and had a modicum of success by picking up more distributors.

We had a change of manufacturer just prior to our next Orlando show and when we received the stock, it was faulty with the bristles falling out and the plastic was very breakable. We were in serious trouble. We received countless complaints and needed to sort out the mess. We went to Brian Steinhobel, an industrial designer of note. He knew and loved our product and was quick to find the solutions to our breaking problems and at the same time give our product the face-lift it sorely required. Jason and Brian worked together and then Jason went to China to do tests with the series 11 Brush-T to make sure that we had a very strong and good product.

Exotic colors were chosen and we had to redesign the packaging as well. We then went back to our first manufacturer.

Jason and Brian then designed a magnificent booth for our re-launch at the Orlando Golf Expo. Jason insisted on handing out sixty-thousand Free Brush-Ts to everyone at the show and we were complimented for putting on one of the best marketing exercises ever seen in Orlando. Paul Krok, our man who runs the American Brush-T has done a superb marketing job as demand is growing day by day, said… *"There was at least one Brush-T in every hotel room in Orlando"*.

The deep faced driver had recently been introduced and there was a demand for a longer Brush-T. Jason designed a double bristle XLT that is over 3" long and is now one of the approved tees for the "long driving contests" that is gaining in popularity throughout the States.

CHAPTER VIII

Over Three-Billion Tees a Year

The Manufacturing, Marketing and Distribution of Golf Tees

The golf tee is vital to the game. A driver costing $450 cannot be effectively used without a tee. Thankfully, the cost of a tee varies from free to five dollars with most recreational purchasers purchasing tees for around $1 for a pack of 10. Most country clubs make tees available at no charge. It's not rare for golfers to "recycle" tees by picking up discarded ones, broken or intact while golfing.

Typically, the longer the tee, the more likely it is to break. On average, golfers use approximately four or five tees per round. Plastic tees are more durable and help alleviate some tee remnant clutter.

Tee-litter

"Pick up your tees and parts as well as other golf tee debris."

There are three course maintenance conditions that require golfer attention and responsibility when playing golf...

1) Repairing ball marks on the green
2) Replacing and/or sanding divots
3) Picking up tee-litter

Dr. Lowell believed his tees should be cheap enough so that a golfer could simply walk away after a tee shot and not retrieve it.

So, he painted the first 5,000 tees green. He quickly learned that most players chose to retrieve and reuse the tee, and green was hard to recover. He quickly changed color painting them red, thus the "Reddy Tee".

Unfortunately, most golfers do treat golf tees as inexpensive replaceable parts of the game. Once a ball has been hit, the golfer's attention follows the ball. That reality has led to broken tee debris cluttering most teeing areas. Unless the tee is easily retrievable, because of its low value and importance, they are quickly abandoned.

Wood tees are responsible for the majority of tee-litter. Over 3 billion wood tees are used each year. The longer the tee, the more likely they are to break. Higher swing speeds increase the breakage factor. On par threes, longer tees hit with irons, break frequently. Using previously broken tees and short stubby tees last longer because they offer less resistance.

Plastic tees offer durability and are nearly unbreakable. Most are lost before they break. Cost is a consideration, which is offset by the reuse of plastics.

Dr. Lowell's 1922 patent also envisioned making the tees with a pressed biodegradable material. And, of course, all wooden tees are ultimately biodegradable

Golf mower equipment manufacturers report that tees cause flat tires, but all course management equipment is designed to easily cut thru tees.

Tee Durability

GOLF TEE TEEOGRAPHY conducted a test using different height tees to determine the longevity of tees made from white birch. We tested seven different tee lengths starting at 1 ½", then increasing to the new 4" maximum length limit imposed by the 2004 USGA rule. Each of the wood tees was inserted into two different turf and soil conditions. One condition was dry and hard and the other was wet and soft. The test used three different swing speeds: 85 mph, 95 mph and 110 mph with 95 mph being the average swing speed for the test.

The result indicated that a golfer can expect to break four to five tees per round (4 par three tees and 14 driver holes). By using the broken tees a second or third time (usually on par 3s) a golfer can expect to use six to eight tees per round. As anticipated, tees broke less with the 85 mph speed than with the 95 mph. Tees broke noticeable more often at the 110 mph speed.

Pride Golf Manufacturing

The Pride Golf Tee Company base in Guilford, Maine produces an estimated 85 per cent of the world production of wood tees and is the dominant marketing force in the tee business. The company was founded in Tampa, Florida where the company originally manufactured wooden cigar tips for Hav-a-Tampa Jewel Cigars.

In 1956, the company moved the business north to Guilford, Maine to be closer to their source of white birch. The wood used for the cigar tips was ideal which made the transition for cigar tips to golf trees an easy one.

The name Pride is perhaps ironic because the company is reticent to reveal much, if anything to the press or public. However, in the industry, they are well known for an excellent fulfillment system. The parent company of Pride is PrideSports which also has interests in cleats (softspikes) and receptacles for the golf industry. PrideSports is based in Gaithersburg, Maryland.

Worldwide production of golf tees is estimated at between two and three billion tees. Pride has mills in Florence, Wisconsin, and Burnham, Maine. Each manufacturing facility produces millions of tees daily; they are made from white birch. Although the company exhibits annually at the PGA Merchandise show in Orlando and has a director of sales and also a director or marketing. The company is generally publicity-shy. However, in a 2003 article that appeared in The Washington Times, Dan Tilton, Pride's sales manager was extensively quoted:

"We've got proprietary equipment, so we're very careful about cameras. The tooling was all made by us. We designed it, and we maintain it with no outside help. That's one of our great advantages. You can't decide you want to start making tees and buy the technology off the shelf."

"We feel very good about our position on the environment. With the cutting laws we have now, basically everybody has to be managing their forests correctly. And one of the unique things about the birch tree is it's considered a weed tree. It's the fastest growing hardwood tree in existence. One of the unique things about the white birch is that it's

fairly solid, but it also has a natural resin in it, which allows us to turn it at a very, very high rate of speed. If, say, you tried to make tees out of maple, you would have to drop oil on the wood while it was turning to keep it from burning. Pine is too soft and would bind and bend. The white birch is the perfect turning wood. You can literally turn hundreds of pieces a minute without any problems."

"It's definitely a high volume, low margin business." Said Tilton, who is enthused about the trend toward the longer tees necessitated by the proliferation of whale-headed driver dominating the equipment industry... "That's the most exciting development in the tee industry in decades."

Pride also produces cigar tips and its product line includes more than 5,000 custom hardwood turnings for the piano, furniture, hardware, household, toy and craft and hobby industries.

Other Tee Manufacturers & Trademarked Tees

WOM Par 3 Tees	Alignmentee
Perfect-Tee	Brush-T
Launcher Tee	Champ FLYtee
Aero-Tees	Pro Tee
Flex Tees	Velocitee
Stinger Golf Tees	Eco Golf Tees
Hi-Per-Tees	Friction-Less
Flexible-Head	TIPS Super Tees

Bio Golf Tees	Certain Tee
Fertile-Tees	XT- 1 Tees
Non-Slice Golf Tees	Twist - Tee
Sur-T	Simarki
Perfect Teez	Super Air Tees
Rocket Tee	Wilson Staff
Zero Friction	Super Air Tees
Smartee	Velocitee Golf Tees
Korectee	Pride Pro
Ti-tees	Koviss Spring Tees
Distanza Tees	XT-1 Tees
Spine Tee	A-Balance Golf Tees
X-Tee	Fancy Tee
Rip Tips	Bazooka
Step Down	One Tee
Rocket Tees	Royal Tees

Many golfers are collectors, accumulating anything from ball markers to rare hand-made golf clubs. Developing a collection of tees is an interesting pursuit. Even though one company

103

manufactures the vast majority of tees, tees still come in various designs, shapes and sizes. Tees also come in different materials, colors and finishes. Collecting tees is perfect for the budget-conscious golf memorabilia collector.

Most serious tee collectors will look for items like prototypes of modern tees; then early antique tees from the 1890s; and then from the 1920s "Tee Patent Frenzy". Some also collect old Golf Tee Boxes and printed Golf Tee Bags.

CHAPTER IX

400 Golf Tees - Classifications

The most basic and prevalent tee is the insertion tee. Early sand mold tee designs have a special interest. I have a collection of over 400 golf tee designs, and I know I've missed a lot.

400 Golf Tee Designs and counting

Following are classifications to spur your interest:

Surface

Insertion

Novel

Foam

Combo

Leaner

Stacker

Funnel

Card T

Cone

Grant

Hook

Metal

Ornamental

Dart

Anchor

Brush

Crown

Variable Height

Tilt Swivel

Tethered

Round

Quad

Cap

Hex

Edge

Naked Lady

Spring Tee

Omni

Mammoth Tooth

Rubber Shield

Pencil / pen

Tee-Head Shapes

Round-Large

Round-Regular

Round-Small

Crown

Edge

Dual

Trip

Quad

Hex

Square

Triangle

Brush

Names for Tees

Most tees do not carry brands or names. As such, they are hard to identify. Some are known only by the name the inventor gave the tee. Without interest and documentation, most inventors fail to finance the manufacturing and marketing efforts of their tees and its history, they simply vanish.

There are more than 1,000 different versions of golf tees.

There are probably as many names as there are tees. Inventors clearly had fun when naming their creations…

Alignmentees – Always Ready – Angle – Daintee – Dodo – Exact-a-tee – Formatee – Go-tee – Holdfast- Infinitee – Launching Pad – Magic – Mightee – Fightee –Never Lose – No Looz – Novel-tee – O-Katy – Par Buster – par-tee – Pencil – Perfec Tee – Perfectum – Perma-tee – Reddy Tee - Rev-Tee - Re – Rite – Rite-Hite – Site-tee – Stay Put – Strip-tees – Target Tee – Tip Top – Tip Not Tee – Tip – Triple – Tripoe – Tru-Drive – Wright-Way - WOM Par 3 Tees.

Golf Tee Classifications

The patented tees of the past one-hundred-twenty years have been classified into SURFACE TEES or INSERTION TEES. There are only two ways to use a tee… place it on the ground or insert it into the ground.

Wood tees are made with lathes or they are pressed. Synthetics are injection molded using plastic, rubber or biodegradable materials. Metal tees are usually stamped, molded, forged, bent or in the case of multiple materials either hand-make or machine assembled.

SURFACE TEES:

Surface tees are set on the ground, grass or a mat. A surface tee may be tethered with an insertion device into the ground and still be classified as a surface tee. Many surface tees are used on mats or at driving ranges. They can also be place directly on hard ground or on the grass. Some have been weighted with lead. They are excellent tees to guarantee proper height of the ball and they usually have a long life and are easily retrievable. Because of the flexibility of injection molding, the shapes can be complex.

Usually made of plastic or rubber, they are separated into two sub-category design groups, Volcano shapes or Freeform shapes.

INSERTION TEES: are separated into four sub-categories: Lathe, Molded, Directional and Combination:

The golfer pushes an insertion into the ground or turf to assure a strong structure to place the ball. Inserted wood tees have accounted for over 99% of all tee use in the past 80 years. Plastic tees do everything that wood tees do and are more durable (resistance to breaking), but they are more expensive. Rubber has been used sparingly. Complex or ornamental designs require injection molding.

CHAPTER X

Golf Ball History

"The ball is the essence of the game"

There is very little definite information as to where golf began, but most agree that golf started along the Eastern Coast of Scotland back in the mid-fifteenth century. It was a favorite game of Kings.

The wooden balls they used were probably made of hardwoods like Beech. Clubs were also made of wood, so the wood to wood crash must have created a resounding sound. Because of its simple shape and material, there is no documentation and no samples of the earlier golf ball, only replications.

The evolution of the Golf Ball included four distinct periods:

140? – **Wooden** (Hardwoods like beech)

1618 – **Feathery** (Feathers stuffed in leather)

1848 – **Gutty** (Gutta-Percha)

1898 – **Rubber-Core**

1932 – **Modern**

In 1618 the **Feathery** was invented and made of goose or chicken feathers stuffed into a cowhide sphere. The process first boiled *"a hat full of feathers"* then it was mashed into a pile of pulp. The leather shrank as it dried and the feathers expanded into compact hard balls. The balls were then painted and sold for prices that often exceeded the cost of clubs. The construction and making of a **Feathery** was expensive and time consuming. So much so, it put the price out of the reach for the majority of potential golfers. It was an exceptional ball with great flight characteristics. It was so much better than the **Wooden** ball that the wooden ball quickly became obsolete. The **Feathery** became the standard of golf balls for the next two hundred thirty years.

In 1848 the Rev. Dr. Robert Adams Paterson made what is believed to be the first "**Gutty**" made from the latex of the Gutta-percha tree from Malaysia. It was a hard brittle ball that became soft and impressable in boiling water. Gutta balls were handmade by rolling around on a table. It was quickly learned that rough balls had better flight characteristics than smooth balls. This lead to Gutta balls with a consistent pattern by a hand-hammer with a sharp edge. Later, metal presses made the balls available at cheaper prices. The balls were usually painted white for general play and red for use in the snow. The most popular Gutty design was *"The Bramble"*, made of small budges, resembling a Brambleberry (Blackberry). Their lower price opened the doors to low-income golfers.

The first <u>hand-cut</u> **Gutty** balls were produced between 1850 – 1875.

The first <u>molded</u> **Gutty** balls were produced between 1875 – 1898.

In 1898 the **Rubber-Core** golf ball was invented by Coburn Haskell, a dentist and a wealthy entrepreneur. Haskell entered into a partnership with the BF Goodrich Company to manufacture and market the ball.

Haskell had driven to Akron from Cleveland to enjoy a round of golf with superintendent of BF Goodrich, Bertram Work. While waiting for Bertram, Haskell wound a long rubber thread into a ball. When he bounced it, it went to the ceiling. When Work saw the rubber ball he suggested putting a cover on it. The new ball was called the Haskell. It had the effect of revolutionizing the game. The new golf ball became the essence of golf. The design featured a sold rubber center with high-tension rubber thread wrapped around it, coated with a gutta-percha cover. Bramble, mesh and reverse mesh designs gave way to the first dimple pattern in 1908. Multiple outer designs were created for better airflow and flight characteristics. Then in 1900 John Gammeter patented the first automatic winding machine, which allowed mass production to economically produce the **Rubber-Core** golf balls. Because there were no standards, ball size and weight varied widely.

On January 1, 1932, USGA standardized the golf ball's weight and size, following the 1930 standard set by the British Golf Association for a slightly smaller ball. In 1990 both R&A and USGA agreed to use the same ball. Today's golf balls are technological wonders that consider: Aerodynamic dimple patterns; Lift – lift is created by the amount of spin that is exerted on the golf ball at impact; Drag – drag is created by the airflow that travels around the ball as it moves from being hit to its final resting spot; Humidity – humidity has a direct effect on the distance of the ball. Warmer climate means the ball will compress to a higher degree, creating more bounce from the clubface; Compression – High speed pictures reveal what happens as a ball is hit. It "compresses" or "loses it shape". Actual contact between the ball and club lasts for on $1/2000^{th}$ of a second. Golf ball manufacture balls with 80, 90 or 100 compression balls to match different swing speeds. The durability and precision of today's golf balls are created by a variety of high-tech advances through the development of space age plastics, silicone and plastics. We now have a two-piece, a three-piece, a four-piece and a five-piece golf ball to choose from.

CHAPTER XI

USGA, R&A and Golf Tee Rules

It is time to bifurcate the rules of golf

The **United States Golf Association** (USGA) and the **Royal and Ancient Golf Club of St. Andrews** (R&A) have demonstrated that they are not good stewards of the world-wide game of golf. It is time to replace them with simpler rules that players of all levels (beginner and profession) of the game can understand.

The current rules are subject to multiple interpretations and decisions. They have constantly been changed. The first written rules of golf in 1744 contained 13 articles. The current rule book is 205 pages and the "Rules Decisions" is a bound two-volume book. Professional Golfers of the PGA do not understand all the rules. Each PGA golf tournament has officials to help interpret each rule decision. Depending upon availability, some decisions create long delays, such as the twenty-minute delay caused by a ball and television cables in a recent Accenture tournament in Tucson. The rules of golf are like IRS rules and can only be interpreted by the governing body with a book (or cell phone) in hand.

The fundamentals of the game should be preserved to protect the spirit and intent of the early rules.

The intent of the rules of the game has always been to protect the integrity of the game and to play the ball as it lies and play the course as you find it.

When the first surface and insertion tees started emerging in the 1890s, the rule-makers paid no attention to the new inventions, probably because, by definition, they were artificial and none of them turned out to have any commercial merit and thus failed to impact the game.

However, the commercial success of the Lowell *"Reddy Tees"*, selling in the millions and its imitators sales meant that the rule-making bodies *had* to have taken notice. In the United States in the 1920s, the body that wrote the rules was the USGA and in the United Kingdom the body was the R&A. Today the USGA and R&A govern golf worldwide with essentially the same rule book. They jointly review and, if necessary, revise the rules every four years.

One of the incidents regarding the new tees took place in the Amateur Championship held at St. Andrews in 1924. One of the competitors, H. D. Gillies, was using a tee that was about six inches long, perhaps longer. He used the long tee because his driver had a huge head. The rules committee posted this notice…

"The Rules Committee hopes that all golfers, before making use of abnormal methods of play or abnormal implements, will earnestly consider whether they are acting in conformity with the spirit of the rule of golf and, in particular, with spirit of the regulations governing the form and make of golf clubs. The Committee considers that it is much to be deplored that players, instead of trying to master the use of

golf clubs, should endeavor to overcome the difficulties of the game by using implements which have never been associated with it."

There is no indication as to whether Mr. Gillies decided against his enormous tee based on the stern edict above. Yet, until 2004, the USGA and the R&A did not author a rule specifically for the tee. However, rules 8-2 and 14-3 usually covered the usability and legality of a tee. Rule 8-2 essentially says that golfers are not allowed to use a device that indicates line of play while making a swing. Rule 14-3 is general but covers the illegality of any device that would help the golfer when making a swing. Until 2004, this rule led tee makers with unique designs to submit the new tee to the USGA for approval.

The Rules of Golf includes plenty about the "teeing".

"In teeing, the ball may be placed on the ground, or an irregularity of surface created by the player on the ground or on a tee, sand or other substance in order to raise it off the ground."

There was no reference to any penalty for infringement.

In 2004, during the quadrennial review and revision of the rules of golf, the USGA and R&A made some major changes to Rule 11. For the first time, the rule makers defined the tee and create a penalty for infractions.

"Tee" (Definition) page 15, 2004 USGA *The Rules of Golf*

"A 'tee' is a device designated to raise the ball off the ground. It must not be longer than 4 inches (101.6 mm) and it must not be designed or

manufactured in such a way that it could indicate the line of play or influence the movement of the ball."

Rule 11-1 concerning "teeing ground", now included these draconian words.

*"In teeing, if a player uses a non-conforming tee or any other object to raise the ball off the ground, **he is disqualified**."*

The USGA and R&A also further defined the teeing ground.

"The 'teeing ground' is the starting place for the hole to be played. It is a rectangular area two club-lengths in depth, the front and the sides of which are defined by the outside limits of two tee-markers. A ball is outside the 'teeing ground' when all of it lies outside the 'teeing ground'."

The 2004 Rule Book was revised to clarify and simplify the rules wherever possible. Kenneth Chapman, a linguistics expert, spent four years correcting bad language and confusing rules. His goal was to create clear conversational language. It would have been additionally useful if he could have condensed the 160 pages back to the original thirteen rules or articles. The current 500 page book titled Decisions on the Rules of Golf is used to interpret its own rule book. Nowhere in either book is the word *"fun"*.

RULE 11.1 DISQUALIFICATION ?

The USGA rule is silly, hypocritical and draconian.

There are <u>three elements</u> to the "**Tee**" (Definition) of Rule 11.1 that was published in the 2004 USGA, *The Rules of Golf*. It was the first time the USGA and R & A tried to define the "tee".

1) <u>The tee must not be longer than 4 inches.</u>
   Why! What can a 4 ¼ inch or 6 inch tee do differently than a 4 inch tee?
2) <u>The tee cannot indicate line of play.</u>
   Lines are allowed on every other piece of golf equipment... Branding iron style putters; golf balls; irons; hybrids and drivers. Why is the tee excluded from assisting alignment?
3) <u>The tee cannot influence the movement of the ball.</u>
   *The purpose for using a tee **is to influence** the movement of the ball by allowing for a clean strike of the ball by the golf club.*

USGA & R & A have gone from totally blinking the tee to a ridiculous definition that includes the penalty of disqualification

The rules of golf are not intended to apply to the use of training aids or practice devices, or their use in casual rounds of golf, which is the majority of all golf played. The USGA Rule 11-1 flies in the face of equity. Why is alignment in the rule concerning tees when it's not mentioned with regards to other golf equipment? Line of play indicators are clearly marked on balls, putters and drivers.

USGA has been inconsistent when it comes to the approval of golf equipment – which is curious because both the USGA and R&A claim that their responsibility is to *"protect the tradition and integrity of golf."*

The USGA allows a putter manufacturer to extend the back of the putter, through the "line-of-the-putt" which "assists in making a stroke." The Rules of Golf allow driver manufacturers to build trampoline faces to influence the "movement of the ball" and to place a line on top of the head, that "indicates line-of-play." The USGA also allows golf ball manufacturers to use new technology that lets the ball stay on the club face longer, go straighter and farther; it lets manufacturer and golfers draw lines on the balls "to indicate line-of-play."

But – the USGA does not allow a tee to indicate line-of-play or assist in making a stroke or influence the movement of the ball. A golf tees sole purpose in raising the ball, to offer a clean strike and to help influence the movement of the ball.

The USGA originally turned down the patented three-ball putter, then approved the two-ball putter from Odyssey, a division of Callaway Golf when it purchased the patent.

Had the governing bodies adhered to their own *"plain in shape"* concept and the *"traditions of golf"* for determining new products, they could have maintained consistency in the game and eliminated lawsuits and controversy concerning: Metal woods; COR; Weird-looking Branding-Iron Putter Heads and Putters that hang from your chin.

Why the sudden interest in the Tee? Did the USGA discover some unknown physical influence attributable to the tee? Is the USGA setting up some type of action on artificial devices or unusual equipment? After 90 years of ignoring the tee, it seems strange that the USGA and the R&A would suddenly write so specific a rule.

The USGA believes and has stated publically, ***our purpose is to protect the game, <u>not grow the game</u>.***

The *"Rules of Golf"* should provide equitable standards for all manufacturers and the use of their equipment during sanctioned play. They should abide by time tested and published standards of *"plain classic design"*.

The difference between the game professionals play and the game amateurs play is significant. It is time to offer a simple set of rules for beginners and amateurs so they do not have to become lawyers or be charged with "cheating" or "breaking the rules". It can be as simple as charging a stroke for touching or moving the ball, once it is in play.

Two out of every three people who try to play golf, give it up.

<u>It is time to bifurcate the rules of golf.</u>

HAVE FUN / ENJOY A GREAT WALK IN THE PARK

CHAPTER XII

USGA Decisions

Shakespeare was right…
"The first thing we do, is kill all the lawyers"

People who make and enforce rules and laws have a self important arrogance about themselves. Somehow, knowing the rules and citing page and verse entitles the official or governing body the interpretive skills to *"be right"* even if the overwhelming view or concept of doing the right thing is wrong. Sometimes, having the authority to interpret the rules is simply given to the wrong people.

Tradition has a special place in our culture. It has a very special place for golf fans dating back centuries when the game was referred to as *"goff"* and played with only few rules.

The rule making organizations R&A and USGA that have been entrusted to manage the game of golf still don't believe that it is their role to *"grow the game"*. The result of their voluminous set of rules and decisions and constantly changing rules has kept many new golfers from the game. The numerous contentious rule violations seen each weekend have left even die-hard golf fans shaking their heads.

For example: the following are golf rules decisions and terms:

"Using a 4 ¼" golf tee" – Disqualification

"Signing a score card when you didn't penalize yourself" – A stroke penalty and DQ.

"Seeing a ball go into a tree and not being able to identify it" – Lost ball – Two stroke penalty

"Loose impediment" – A two-ton boulder in Phoenix – The crowd moving it – No Penalty

"Building a stance" – Placing a towel under the knees. – Signing a wrong scorecard because you didn't penalize yourself - DQ

"Moving a leaf while making a stroke" – A penalty violation

"Signing a scorecard with more strokes than you took" – Disqualification at the Masters.

"Your ball hits you" – A stroke penalty

"Your ball strikes your equipment or caddie" – A stroke penalty

"Helping or Telling where to hit the ball" – A stroke penalty

"Falling with a club in a hazard" – A stroke penalty

"Grounding your club at Whistling Straits in a crowd" – A stroke penalty

"Slow play" – A foreign 14 year old playing at the Masters for the first time. A stroke penalty.

In 2003 my **ALIGNMENTEE**TM invention, an insertion-tee with a collapsing pointer was sent to USGA for approval before going to the expense of patenting, manufacturing and marketing it. USGA denied the tee design saying it was "non-conforming". This was one year before they published the 2004 Rule 11.1 that made it a disqualification to use a tee that indicates line-of-play.

In 2009 the **WOM**TM **Par 3 Tee** invention was sent to USGA for approval prior to patent, manufacturing and marketing. The **WOM** surface-tee design features colorful twisted pipe-cleaners that can easily be set on the ground, out of sight, then retrieved, reshaped and reused. **USGA denied the application, stating that it was not a** *"tee"*. (The definition of a tee is *"A stand to support a stationary ball"*.) It clearly is a *"tee"*.

Non-Decision: Jack Nicklaus 15th Hole Augusta

On the par five 15th hole at the Masters, Jack Nicklaus hit his second shot hole high on the side of a knoll pin high. It landed next to a chair. As Jack removed the chair the ball rolled toward the green. Having marked the ball, Jack retrieved the ball and replaced it in play. Then as Jack walked down toward the hole, the ball released again and rolled down onto the green. Jack then picked the ball up and took it to the spot he had originally placed the ball. He then played out the hole. According to the rules of golf Jack should have left the ball on the green. Jack did what was right in the spirit of the game when he replaced the ball. It was the honorable thing to do but it violated the rules. Jack should have been penalized for playing the ball in the wrong position and ultimately disqualified for signing a wrong score card as was Craig Stadler in a later tournament

Decision: Craig Stadler 14th Hole Torrey Pines

During the playing of the 1987 San Diego Open at Torrey Pines, Craig Stadler placed a towel to protect his slacks as he kneeled to make a shot under a tree. After hitting the shot a viewed called in and complained that Craig had *"built a stance"* in violation of the rules. Stadler was disqualified for signing an incorrect score card because he did not assess himself a penalty stoke.

Decision: Tiger Woods - Phoenix Open

A large two-ton boulder impeded Tiger Wood's swing. Two hundred fans took it upon themselves to move the bolder. The rules officials claimed the bolder was a *"loose impediment"* and that there was no penalty and the moving of the boulder was interpreted evenly...

Even if the boulder rule was applied correctly, Woods should not have allowed it. Technically, it may not have been a violation of the rules but it was a violation of the spirit of the game.

Decision: Dustin Johnson, 18th Hole US Open Whistling Straights

After playing from what he believed to be a sandy area, surrounded by fans, Dustin was assessed a stroke penalty for grounding his club in a sand hazard. The penalty kept him out of a playoff and a chance to win the Open.

What other USGA Championship allows fans to stand in and/or walk thru sand traps?

So, moving a loose impediment like a two-ton rock is OK with no penalty and dislodging a leaf or moving a leaf while swinging includes a penalty stroke???

Or touching the loose sand with your club with a crowd standing all around you is a penalty because USGA so ruled??? Why would USGA allow spectators to stand in sand traps at a US Open championship?

CHAPTER XIII

New Rules of Golf...
Return to the original "13 Articles of Golf".

Clearly, there are two games of golf... the game the PGA professionals play and the game the beginner-amateur plays. And of course, there are the notable exceptional amateur golfers like Bobby Jones who have had a huge influence on how a great amateur can compete with pros. The huge purses and contracts the sport generates guarantee there will always be a semi-pro group of "want-a-bees" that will separate themselves from the amateur ranks with an eye on becoming professionals.

The PGA and television have created sporting events with exceptional entertainment value and following. They support an entire manufacturing and marketing industry. Its weak link has been the USGA and R&A rules violations and interpretations that border on the ridiculous. The USGA set-up of courses for majors like Whistling Straights in Wisconsin and Shinnecock in New York are extreme examples of USGA self-importance where amateurs tell professionals how the game should be played. It is time for the PGA to determine the rules that will guide their play and further help them *"grow the game"*.

The life blood of any business is new blood.

Bifurcate the rules

All golf should **play the course** as the golfers find it.

The ball should be **played as it lies**.

The rules **do not need to be constantly changed.**

Golf should be **fun and encouraging**.

Golf rules for the beginner-amateurs should be short enough and simple enough to fit on scorecards. The 13 Articles of Golf can be as simple as - *"NO TOUCH GOLF"*. If you touch or move your ball, add a stroke. Out-of-bounds, one-stroke. In a hazard, one-stroke to take it out. Behind a tree or bush, move it so you have a shot, one-stroke. On a path, either play it, or move it, one-stroke.

As to equipment - change back to the basic **plain in shape** rule.

Fundamentally, the game should be played by doing what is right. Arguing over rules interpretations or correcting someone for unknowingly "breaking the rules" is not in the spirit or tradition of the gentlemanly game of **goff**.

The intent of the rules has always been to protect the integrity of the game; to play the golf course as you find it; and to play the ball as it lies.

CHAPTER XIV

WOM PAR 3 GOLF TEES

"Use it 'til you lose it!"

RETRIEVE IT – RE-SHAPE IT – RE-USE IT

No broken tees – No sharp points – No tee-litter

Hitting the *"Sweet spot"* on irons between the 5th and 7th groove produces the most consistent repeatable ball-striking.

WOM PAR 3 TEES are made of Classic White or multiple colored NEON twisted pipe stems. They can be custom-tied with custom color schemes. They are easy to find – most **WOM** tees will travel about 28 ½ feet directly to the front. Created for Par 3 holes, they work equally well with Hybrids and 3-Woods.

WOMs are easily carried in pockets or on the top-rim of a golf visor. As surface tees, they are alternatives to insertion tees with hard ground conditions or mats.

Each **WOM** surface tee is hand-tied. As such, there will always be slight variations. Minor adjustments may be needed to assure the ball sits securely. Both ends of **WOMs** are slightly larger to help support the ball. After hitting and retrieving a **WOM,** it will need to be reshaped to its circular form. This is easily accomplished by using the shaft of a club, pencil or pen to rewind the **WOMs** to its original circular shape.

WOM PAR 3 TEES "conform" to current Rule 11.1 of USGA and R&A regulations for golf tees: USGA says they do not.

1) <u>They do not indicate line-of-play</u> - They are invisible while addressing the ball.
2) <u>They **do** influence the movement of the ball</u> – The purpose of a tee is to influence the movement of the ball. The ball sits lightly on the fuzzy surface of pipe stems.
3) <u>The tee must not be longer than 4 inches</u> – A WOM is only 3 inches long when stretched out.

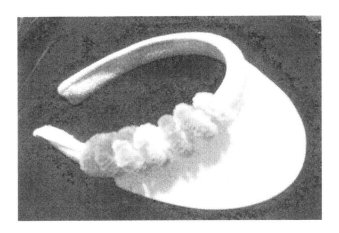

WOM Golf Visor Caddy

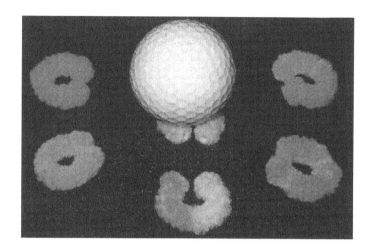

Instructions to tie custom **WOM Par 3 Tees** can be purchased for $10 at <u>WOMpar3tees.com</u>

CHAPTER XV

TEECUTTER

Improving upon the Classic Lowell Tee design that has been used for over ninety years will be nearly impossible because of its acceptance and use worldwide. It is a nearly perfect solution for a golf tee design. The major hurdle every inventor will have to overcome is the cost factor since many wooden tees are given free or picked up from previous use. Free is a huge hurdle for entrepreneurs.

Still, the concept of the tee being used 3,000,000,000 times a year suggests that if someone were to get just a small piece of that pie, it would be worthwhile to try and find that gap analysis opportunity.

Wooden tees have three areas of weakness:

1) **Friction** – Mechanical swing machines have tested multiple new golf tee designs, the majority of which were plastic or combinations of different materials. In each case the classic wooden tee was the standard of comparison, and each time the plastic golf tee head with less surface contact with golf ball proved that friction was a factor that affected the direction and distance of the golf ball.

2) **Broken Tees** – Longer wooden tees, larger driver heads and irons with increased club head swing speed break most wooden tees. Shorter more compact tees have longer lives. Many broken tees are reused. Some have their rough

broken ends sharpened with a pocket knife. Some broken ends can still be inserted into the ground.

3) **Tee Litter** – Abandoned, lost and broken wooden tees account for the majority of the tee litter. An increased awareness of the problem and reuse of broken tees are partial solutions.

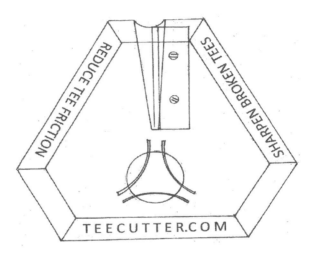

The New TEECUTTER addresses each issue of wooden tee weakness. It is a device to be carried in a golfers pocket to cut and remove 75% to 85% of the mass of the head of a wooden golf tee and still maintain the golf ball stability on the tee. It reduces the amount of friction between the tee and the golf ball caused by the force of the club striking the ball thereby, reducing deflection and increasing accuracy and the distance the golf ball travels.

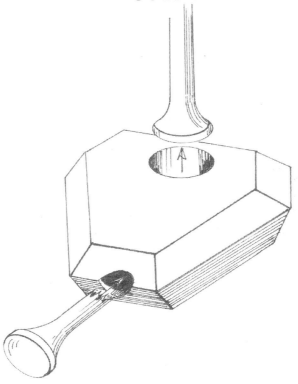

The TEECUTTER is a small 2 ¼″ triangle shape with squared off points. It has two major unique features:

1) **Wooden Golf Tee Friction Reducer**

   Three curved blades are placed on a wooden golf tee with its head on a solid flat surface. Once positioned over the curved finger grip that leads to the head of the tee, pressure is applied evenly on both sides of the TEECUTTER to easily cut three portions from the head of the tee.

133

2) Wooden Golf Tee Sharpener

The tee sharpener restores the point of a broken tee by simply rotating the head of the tee with the fingers until it reaches the desired sharpness, while the other hand holds the TEECUTTER

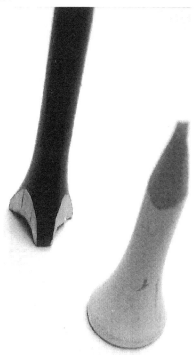

Currently, wooden tees do not offer the feature of reduced friction heads. Plastic tees offer various friction reduction head shapes, but at greatly increased costs. Most sharpening of wooden tees for reuse are whittled points using a pocket knife.

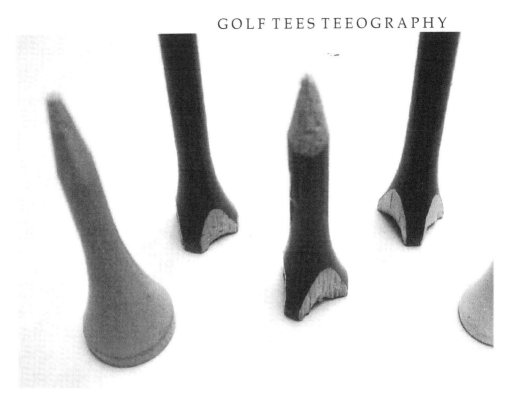

The TEECUTTER has multiple other uses:

It can be used as an advertising specialty item to promote a brand, product or service. I can be used as a scorecard pencil sharpener or a marker. It will hold you club dry off the ground when the grass is wet. The TEECUTTER can clean grooves and shoes and also scrape ice off windshields.

CHAPTER XVI

"Tee it down" by Robert Trent Jones, II

There are a number of passionate individuals who are unhappy and concerned with the direct technology is taking the game of golf. Many believe the game should be bifurcated into separate rules… one set for professionals and another for amateurs.

Some believe courses are too long, too expensive to maintain and take too long to play. Others are concerned with cost of equipment and play. They suggest restricting the distance the ball will travel, limiting driver designs, shortening courses and even eliminating the golf tee.

For three quarters of a century, the Jones name has signified imaginative, well-crafted golf course designs. Demonstrating creativity and professionalism in equal degree, Robert Trent Jones, Sr. shaped the modern craft of golf course architecture. Robert Trent Jones, Jr. – a lifetime member and former President of the American Society of Golf Course Architects – has expanded his father's legacy, founding an innovative modern golf course design firm with a global reach and a reputation of creating value.

Following are excerpts from *"Tee it down"* dinner as presented by Robert Trent Jones, II to the American Society of Golf Course Architects at their annual meeting in Santa Barbara, California, April 28, 2002.

"Tee it down!"

Last year at the U.S. Open at Southern Hills in Tulsa, I had the privilege to be included in an informal discussion at a private dinner hosted by the USGA. The discussion turned on how traditional championship course could stand up against the onslaught of ball and implement technology. Thus, I now report to you a proposal made by Peter Dawson, Secretary of the R&A at that time, with which I concur.

"There's one sure way to level the playing field of golf." The Wise Man said. "And that is to take away the current artificiality. Your don't have to ban any new technology. You don't require the player to give up his preferred ball with its *hexogumple* dimples and its *hoxadymonic* flight pattern. Your don't even have to fight a patent. The only patent pertaining to my subject has long expired. *"We also have a long-standing tradition on which to base our decision. **It's called playing the ball as it lies**,"* Mr. Dawson reminds us.

So colleagues, here's the plan: ***"We ban the tee from the tee."***

Each club player will be allowed to roll his ball around on that area, praying that he find a tuft of something, or a worm cast, or an acorn-cup or whatever, while our job will be to ensure that each tee is properly constructed to be tightly cut and a smooth and fine as any eleven stimp-measured green. But during club medals or other championships, the rule would be simple. Drop the ball between and behind the markers and play it from where it comes to rest.

There will be one new etiquette standard, and that shall be all. A player who scuffs the teeing area will be required to make repairs from available sod and sand to ensure the area is left as pristine as we presently leave bunkers and greens. With that, then let the best player find some way to fly the ball with a 7.5 degree light-alloy, bigheaded driver three hundred and thirty-three yards through the air.

And for my fellow golf course architects in the audience we shall have a role to play in all of this. Up until now most of you have moving bunkers on the fairway wings forward from two hundred and sixty yards out into the high tow eighties. Now I want you to consider placing sizable bunkers with significant lips, and very soft, powdery sand, say about fifty to one-hundred yards, or so from the championship tees as Donald Ross once implemented.

I see some of your grimacing, no doubt thinking that this change will only serve to take the driver out of the hands of highly-skilled exponents of golf; and that they would simply use 3-wood to get ample distance, the way young Tiger Woods has done in order to master holes such as that tough, dogleg 13th at Augusta National with a high sweeping hook. Perhaps therefore I have not been sufficiently explicit in the proposal.

What I heard is exactly the opposite: the driver will still be obligatory for everyone on the par fours and fives. The only other option permitted will be the wedge. Draconian, did I hear someone murmur? Perhaps, but you see we have sat around for long enough doing nothing while that was always the constant complaint. No, we have waited for far too long while technology crept up on us and turned golf on its ear. Now it is impossible to turn back the clock, and we are struck with lawsuits by manufacturers, and how resistance to change is bad for the game and on an' on.

Nevertheless, now we can do something and something very positive, even though it too will cause some measure of resentment. Still, that's the way things have always been with golf, ever since Old Tom Morris or even before his time.

Our own historian Geoff Cornish and some older members of the audience will probably recall reading about the acrimonious feud between feathery ball maker Allan Robertson and Old Tom Morris. It was so contentious that Old Tom moved his club-making and teaching business across the entire width of Scotland from St. Andrews to Prestwick. Morris favored the new guttie ball, a product that would have Robertson out of business, had he not been decent enough to die first. That ball changed golf, and most say for the better, and perhaps that is hard to dispute because the easier, cheaper guttie attracted more players to the game.

But, fifty years later, the next-generation ball – that bouncing, bounding Haskell – was not viewed by top professional players as an improvement. The great harry Vardon, after his first test, stated the new ball would make the game too simple and particularly decried the loss of one skill, "Playing the guttie into a tough headwind," Vardon wrote, "has always been the toughest shot in the game." Learning to strike down on the ball

139

to ensure it does not bellow up and finish behind you was an art. Sadly this new ball has taken all the risk out of that shot. "Thus the sand patty tee mound became more in vogue to help get the ball airborne." (Subsequently Vardon, the most talented player of his era accepted a lucrative tour of the United States to promote this new ball.) Innovations, good and bad, were arriving thick and fast at the end of the nineteenth century. Among them the original greens mower provide the first consistently maintained putting surfaces. Dr. George Franklin Grant, graduate of the Harvard School of Dentistry, class of 1870, spent most of his nineteen-nineties leisure time on the recently imported fad of golf. Perhaps he was the persnickety fellow accustomed to permanently clean hands. Whatever the reason, he tired of making mud-pie tees from damp sand, he returned to his study and invented golf's first artificial aid. Patent #638,920 was granted in 1899, a ball-perch around two inches tall, a folding rubber top on a upright stem. An immediate success? Not at all. Grant died in 1910, his tee-up idea was shelved a decade earlier from lack of general interest.

The tee-it-up business and dentistry would appear to have no obvious connection, but the next and considerable more successful attempt to put the golf ball on an artificial pedestal was the brainchild of yet another dentist, Dr. William Lowell from Maplewood, New Jersey.

Lowell first experimented with gutta percha, the material use to produce the rubber "guttie" ball, but found the material too brittle. Local birch-wood proved more durable and he painted a trial batch green. Wrong! Red turned out to be the color that caught on and in time all "Reddy Tees" became a vogue. Walter Hagen helped the cause when he accepted a healthy fee from the inventor to publicize the product. Unlike Grant, or perhaps because Grant's patent was still viable, Lowell failed to register his product. Soon the burgeoning golf-market was flooded with imitations.

The artificial peg itself would change very little in the next eight years, outlasting hickory shafts, the stymie, leather wraparound grips, the British ban on center-shafted putters, persimmon drivers, golf hats and shirts without logos and yellow bell-bottomed pants. So please, if you will, concentrate on that word, artificial. Because that is what a tee is, an artifice, a ploy to simplify the game. A Scam invented by the high-handicap player to help get the ball in the air. Golf, my friends, should be properly played, from the ground – to the ground – into the ground.

Here's a bit of history. The "T" is an ancient Egyptian surveyors' mark, set in the ground, meaning "begin here", in the direction of the stem of the "T". But begin what? – A pyramid? – Or begin playing the Royal and Really Ancient game.

To my knowledge, only two entrepreneurial types made personal fortunes from tee-related matters. Naturally one was a frugal Scot, Hamish MacFadgen, who invented the woolie-bobble, a sort of sporran tassel, but made from knitting wool of various colors, was attached by a piece of tough thread, about a foot in length, to the tee-stem.

141

"Aye. I know it cost sixpence when the tee only cost thrupence. But you'll need ane o'each in lifetime of golf," he'd tell his parsimonious clients.

MacFadgen woolie-bobbles sold in the millions until Grandma Gourlie discovered, much by accident that bobbles were easily and cheaply made at home simply by means of twisting and knotting excess knitting yarn and so ended MacFadgen's fortune.

The sprawling British Empire introduced the game of golf to India long before it reached New York and Jamil "Pindle" Singh – so nicknamed for the paucity of his drives – also made a small fortune from the game. Aware that the ownership of a tiger's tooth was considered one of the most significant of all good-luck charms in his native land, he inventively added superstition to his sales pitch. Boring a small hole in each large tiger-tooth, he threaded a small wire through the hole and attached the other end to a wooden tee; a ploy by which he persuaded gullible clients that they could always find their tee and have good fortune at the same time. Such aids are now but a footnote in the litany of golfing memorabilia, while the artificial tee live dangerously on. It is time to kill it before it kills the classic courses we know and love.

Of course there will be a minority who say we are changing the nature of the game by limiting freedom of choice. Yet, we have most certainly done this before. Name me one golf course where a player, whether professional or amateur, is allowed to use any club other than a putter on the greens? Yet once upon a time the tee-off area was from alongside the previous hole, and there was small difference to be noted.

Finally, we have Big Bertha and the little ball. Those who swing ever larger-headed drivers will set the ball upon even higher pegs. Today's young college "limber backs" are already swinging from their heels every time because the physical properties of the metal drive have overcome Hogan's fear of the hook with his persimmon woods. But drop the ball on the ground and the large trampoline sweet spot will physically be above the ball as it lies and therefore useless. Get to the root cause and the new equipment will revert automatically to its former size.

And for all you architects who like to crack eggs to make fresh omelets, you will have plenty of design work to do. For example, you could even design, Tom Fazio did, a *"tee-less"* golf course with the short 10-hole replica course at Pine Valley. Let your imagination be your guide to help save the game.

Ladies and gentlemen, one simple decision today can change golf forever, for the good of all...

"Ban the artificial tee from the game and do it now!"

Robert Trent Jones, II is a history major with a passion and appreciation for the detail in the roots and tradition of golf. He is also a realist who understands the games' intricacies and politics. He understands the influence of the golf ball and club manufacturers and the potentially litigious nature of new product design introductions.

His speech given to other golf course architects was a realistic approach to controlling the length of drive and the future of the game of golf. It is a solution that considers the tradition; the rule makers – USGA, R&A and the PGA; golf equipment manufacturers; and both amateur and professional golfers. Jones and Peter Dawson, then Secretary of R&A, realize that *"Banning the tee"* from golf is an unrealistic expectation given the tees undeniable acceptance and use. But, if equipment continues to allow golfers to hit the ball farther, the result will be longer courses. It will create longer playing times, higher construction costs, higher maintenance costs and more expensive greens fees.

A golf course takes approximately three years to plan, design and build ready to play. Currently, during that time, changes in equipment design happen so quickly that placing a fairway trap five yards differently could make a change on a Robert Trent Jones, Jr. designed course.

The average driving distance for PGA pros has increased 30 yards since 1980. 83% of that increase has come in the past twenty years from an average of 262 yards in 1994 to 286 yards in 2003. Oversize titanium drivers and new balls, designed to complement the new drivers (which ended the wound ball in

2001) and ball launch monitor have all played a part in the increases. More emphasis on physical conditioning has also played a role.

Fun, innovative solutions, cost and public acceptance will determine future golf course designs and the future growth of golf.

EPOLOGUE:

I hope you have enjoyed the journey **GOLF TEE TEEOGRAPHY** has taken you. The tee is a small but very significant part of the marvelous game of golf. Over the past hundred years it has been taken for granted and blinked by USGA & R&A. As such, its history has been unattended.

We've traveled from 1457 with King James the II of Scotland and his archers; thru *"goat tracks"*; to sand and dirt tees at Edinburgh and its original 13 Rules of Golf; to St Andrews and its 18 holes; and to the first tee patent of any type, mould or otherwise by Bloxsom/Douglas; to Dr. George Grant and his rubber and wood tee patent and ultimately to Dr. William Lowell Sr. and the *"Reddy Tee"* and the award winning *"Brush-T"* and it's world- wide marketing efforts.

Over the past one-hundred and twenty-years 400 golf tees designs have kept entrepreneurs awake trying to get a piece of what is now an annual three-billion golf tee market.

Golf's governing bodies appear to have finally accepted *"artificial"* tees. It took them eighty years. They still appear to be reluctant to let new tees into their game.

I don't claim to have written a complete account of the golf tee or the *"wooden peg"*, I have spent ten years putting what information I could find together. I am very happy to have had the input from Joan Lowell Smith (the Lowell family historian) to help document what actually happened with her families efforts

146

to market the *"Reddy Tee"* and acknowledge it's important place in golf's history.

Dr. Lowell Smith Jr. solved a problem. He did not like the untidiness of teeing a golf ball using wet sand and dirt. He had no prior knowledge of golf patents or the rules of golf as they might relate to developing his new invention. During the early stages he did not know that his new tee was considered *"artificial"* by the rules of golf. As he started marketing it, he learned that some viewed it as "illegal", but he forged on because golfers liked them and paid for them. Today, ninety years later, the majority of tees used in golf worldwide use his criteria and his wooden tee design. He opened the door to the golfing world of artificial tees. His fastidious nature made him analyze all the elements that would be required of a tee to replace the natural sand and dirt tees. The result, he created a *"Classic Tee"* that has stood the test of time.

"Growing the game" will require attention to the rules for beginners and amateurs… I wish Dr. Lowell was still around, he would solve the problem.

Thank you.

Have fun golfing with your new found little friend…

Ken Jacobson

Ken Jacobson

Author Profile:

Ken Jacobson is the inventor of the **WOM**TM **Par 3 Tee**, a new surface tee made of bright colorful pipe stems. There is no known tee similar, either in design or construction. It has all the benefits of the Classic Lowell insertion tee design with the added benefits of being *re-coverable, re-shapeable and re-useable*. The tee nests on the ball on air, out of sight, is safe, and offers reduced tee interference.

He is also the inventor or the **TEECUTTER**TM, a device to reduce friction on wooden golf tees heads and sharpen broken tees for reuse.

As an inventor, artist and golfer Ken started collecting golf tee designs when, as a former patent illustrator, he discovered there were over 250 golf tee patents in the United States and more in the United Kingdom. Today, he has collected over 400 individual designs.

Mr. Jacobson is a retired advertising executive who spends his time chasing rainbows in the sky and in the water. He enjoys a *"wandering star life-style"* doing what he wants to when he wants to do it with his Brittany "Gink". He is a member of Wayne Golf Course with an 8 handicap in Bothell, Washington, where he runs "Gink" on goose-patrol after each round of golf.

As a former graphic designer; artist; sculptor; ad-man and inventor, Jacobson is also a bird dog, hunting and gun activist.

He was a member of the 1960 Semi-pro National Championship Cheney Studs; a member of the University of Washington 1959 Baseball Team Hall of Fame and was elected into the American Brittany Club Hall of Fame. He also owned National American & Canadian Dual Champion Pacolet Cheyenne Sam – The only dog of any breed to win its breed National Championship and it National Specialty. Sam is also the only Brittany to compete against pointers and setters and win the (three-hour) International Endurance Shooting Dog Championship.

He is creator of "CRAB BAIT & HAIRBALL", a cartoon that features a Brittany; an erotic cat; "Mo", a bright mouse; "Dirt", a rat that has been given a bad rap simply because he's a rat, and "Boss" who believes the gangs "Cat and Mouse" charade.

He is also the author of the humorous POLITICALLY CORRECT HUNTING and J A C O D E, a factoid journey of the manipulation of man.